The latest UK Ninja Air Fryer Cookbook for Beginners

Super-easy and Time-Saving Ninja Air Fryer Recipes You Will Love for Every Occasion with Expert Tips & Tricks / Collection of Family Favourites

Dina A. Warner

Contents

Chapter 5: Fish and Seafood 25

Chapter 6: Meat and Poultry Dishes 32

Chapter 7: Pizzas, Wraps, and Sandwiches 39

Chapter 8: Appetisers and Side Dishes 47

Chapter 9: Vegan and Veggie 54

Chapter 10: Sweet Treats and Desserts 64

Chapter 1: Air Fryer Basic Guide

As we embark on this culinary journey together, I am thrilled to welcome you to the world of air frying—the realm where convenience meets delectable dishes. With each page, I intend to make your experience not only educational but also incredibly enjoyable.

Allow me to introduce myself—I'm a devoted food enthusiast who, much like you, finds solace and creativity in the kitchen. Cooking, for me, has always been a conduit to expressing love and care for my dear ones. Through this cookbook, I hope to not just share recipes but to forge a connection, making you feel like a cherished member of my culinary circle.

In our pursuit of mastering the Ninja air fryer, I am here to offer guidance, encouragement, and my personal insights. It's not just about crispy fries and succulent chicken; it's about building confidence in your cooking journey. I'm here to hold your hand through each step, ensuring that you feel as though you're cooking right alongside a friend.

Remember, every dish has a story, and I can't wait for you to create your own with the help of this cookbook. So, as you flip through these pages, embrace the excitement of trying something new and revel in the joy of creating magic in your kitchen. Together, let's dive into the world of air frying and make memories that will last a lifetime.

Getting to Know Air Fryers

In our quest to conquer the culinary landscape with the Ninja air fryer, it's crucial to lay down the foundation by understanding the marvel that is the air fryer. Think of it as a culinary wizard that wields the power to transform your dishes into crispy, golden perfection—without the guilt of excessive oil consumption.

So, what exactly is an air fryer? At its core, it's a countertop appliance that harnesses the magic of hot air circulation to cook food to perfection. Much like a mini convection oven, it employs a rapid air technology that circulates superheated air around your food, creating a crispy outer layer while preserving the tenderness within.

The process is remarkably simple yet revolutionary. The air fryer's heating element warms up the air within the cooking chamber, and a powerful fan ensures even distribution of this heated air. As the air circulates, it encounters the food from all angles, causing the Maillard reaction—a chemical process that lends the appetising golden-brown colour and a distinctive flavour to your dishes.

One of the most remarkable aspects of the air fryer is its ability to reduce oil usage significantly. While traditional frying methods require generous amounts of oil to achieve that crispy texture, air frying demands only a fraction of it. This means you can savour your favourite fried treats with far fewer calories and less mess to clean up afterward.

As you delve deeper into this cookbook, keep in mind the marvel of the air fryer—the modern kitchen sidekick that's about to revolutionise the way you cook. With a newfound understanding of its mechanics, you're now ready to embark on a culinary adventure that promises tantalising textures, delightful flavours, and a healthier way to enjoy your favourite meals.

Why is the Air Fryer so Popular?

In recent years, the air fryer has achieved a level of popularity that's nothing short of remarkable. Its rise to culinary stardom can be attributed to a combination of factors that have resonated with modern home cooks and health-conscious food enthusiasts alike.

- **Healthier Cooking Options:** The allure of the air fryer lies in its ability to produce crisp and flavorful

results with significantly less oil compared to traditional deep frying. Health-conscious individuals have embraced this technology as a way to enjoy their favourite fried foods with reduced fat content, making it a game-changer for those striving for a balanced lifestyle.

- **Time Efficiency:** Our fast-paced lives often demand meals that are both quick and delicious. The air fryer steps up to the plate by drastically cutting down cooking times. The rapid hot air circulation ensures that dishes cook faster than conventional ovens, making it an ideal solution for busy individuals and families.
- **Versatility in Cooking:** Beyond its frying capabilities, the air fryer showcases impressive versatility. It's not just for frying; it's a multipurpose kitchen companion that can grill, roast, bake, and even reheat leftovers. Its adaptability makes it an attractive addition to any kitchen.
- **Easy Cleanup:** Traditional frying often results in oily messes and lingering odours. The air fryer, on the other hand, minimises these inconveniences. With its contained cooking environment, there's less splatter, and many parts are dishwasher-safe, making cleanup a breeze.
- **Compact Design:** Modern kitchens come in all shapes and sizes, and the air fryer's compact footprint suits a range of living spaces. Its countertop presence doesn't just save space; it also adds a touch **of contemporary flair to kitchens.**
- **Crave-Worthy Results:** Perhaps the most compelling reason for the air fryer's popularity is the undeniable quality of the dishes it produces. Whether it's perfectly golden French fries or succulent chicken wings, the air fryer delivers

results that are undeniably delicious.

In essence, the air fryer's popularity can be attributed to its ability to align with the evolving needs and preferences of today's culinary enthusiasts. As we delve into the recipes ahead, you'll experience firsthand why this kitchen marvel has become a staple in countless homes around the world.

The Difference Between an Air Fryer and Deep Frying

When it comes to achieving that irresistible crispy exterior, two cooking methods take the stage: air frying and deep frying. While both methods aim to create that satisfying texture and flavour, they do so in strikingly different ways. Let's delve into the nuances and practical implications of each approach.

Cooking Method

Air Frying: Air frying utilises rapidly circulating hot air to cook food. The air fryer's compact cooking chamber ensures that the hot air envelops the food from all angles, resulting in even cooking.

Deep Frying: Deep frying, on the other hand, submerges food in a large quantity of hot oil. The food cooks through direct contact with the oil, which conducts heat efficiently.

Oil Usage

Air Frying: One of the star attractions of air frying is its ability to significantly reduce oil usage. In most cases, only a thin layer of oil is required to achieve a crispy exterior.

Deep Frying: Deep frying demands a substantial amount of oil for successful results. The food needs to be fully immersed in the oil, leading to higher oil absorption.

Texture and Taste

- **Air Frying:** Air frying excels in creating a crisp outer layer while retaining moisture within the food. The result is a lighter texture that allows the natural flavours to shine.
- **Deep Frying:** Deep frying tends to produce a thicker and crunchier crust due to the higher oil content. However, the extensive oil absorption can sometimes overshadow the inherent flavours of the food.

Cooking Time

- **Air Frying:** Thanks to the rapid air circulation, air frying generally requires less cooking time compared to deep frying.
- **Deep Frying:** Deep frying may take longer due to the time it takes for the oil to heat up and the food to cook through the oil.

Cleanup

- **Air Frying:** Air fryers make cleanup hassle-free. The contained cooking environment minimises oil splatters, and many air fryer components are dishwasher-safe.
- **Deep Frying:** Deep frying can lead to messy kitchens with oil splatters on countertops and stovetops. Additionally, disposing of used frying oil requires careful handling.

Let's take a classic comfort food like chicken wings. When air frying, you'd toss the wings in a light coat of oil or even use a cooking spray. The result would be wings with a delightfully crisp skin and tender meat inside. In deep frying, you'd fully submerge the wings in hot oil, resulting in a richer, crunchier exterior but with a higher caloric and fat content. The choice between the two methods ultimately depends on your preference for texture, flavour, and the health-consciousness of your culinary approach.

As you embark on your culinary journey with the air fryer, keep in mind the distinctions between these methods. Whether you're aiming for a healthier twist or seeking that indulgent crunch, the air fryer and deep frying offer distinct avenues to culinary delight.

The Advantages of an Air Fryer

The air fryer, a modern kitchen marvel, has garnered immense popularity for reasons that extend far beyond its ability to produce crispy and delicious dishes. Let's explore the multifaceted advantages that make the air fryer an indispensable tool in your culinary arsenal.

Healthier Cooking without Compromise

Perhaps the most celebrated advantage of the air fryer is its capacity to create dishes with a fraction of the oil traditionally required for deep frying. This reduction in oil usage translates to lower calorie intake and a decreased intake of unhealthy fats. Indulging in favourites like French fries or chicken tenders becomes a guilt-free pleasure, aligning perfectly with those seeking a healthier lifestyle.

Retention of Nutrients and Flavor

Air frying is akin to a culinary magician that manages to lock in the flavours and nutrients of your ingredients while achieving that coveted crunch. By cooking food quickly and at high temperatures, the air fryer ensures that the natural goodness of your ingredients remains intact, resulting in dishes that not only taste fantastic but also nourish your body.

Time Efficiency Redefined

In the fast-paced world we live in, time is a precious commodity. The air fryer's rapid air circulation expedites the cooking process, significantly reducing cooking times when compared to traditional ovens or stovetops. Weeknight dinners are transformed from elaborate affairs to quick, satisfying meals without compromising on taste or quality.

Versatility Unleashed

Beyond its prowess in frying, the air fryer is a versatile wizard that wears many hats. From roasting vegetables and baking bread to grilling seafood and reheating leftovers, it's an all-in-one solution that caters to a diverse array of culinary needs. This adaptability saves both time and kitchen space, making it a true kitchen powerhouse.

Taming the Kitchen Chaos

The contained cooking environment of the air fryer minimises the mess often associated with traditional frying. With little to no oil splattering, cleanup becomes a breeze. Many air fryer components are dishwasher-safe, allowing you to spend more time enjoying your culinary creations and less time scrubbing pots and pans.

Energy Efficiency

Compared to large ovens, the air fryer is an energy-efficient alternative. Its compact size and focused heating method mean it requires less energy to reach and maintain cooking temperatures. This not only reduces your carbon footprint but also trims down your energy bills.

Culinary Confidence Booster

Cooking with the air fryer is a journey of exploration and experimentation. The simplicity of its operation, along with its consistent results, boosts your culinary confidence. As you master various recipes, you'll find yourself stepping into the role of a confident home chef, surprising your loved ones with restaurant-quality dishes.

In essence, the air fryer isn't just a cooking appliance; it's a lifestyle enhancer. It's the gateway to healthier eating, time-efficient cooking, and culinary creativity.

As you continue to delve into the recipes ahead, you'll discover firsthand the limitless possibilities that the air fryer brings to your kitchen, transforming everyday cooking into an extraordinary experience.

How to Choose the Right Air Fryer?

With the myriad of air fryers available on the market, finding the perfect one for your kitchen can be a gratifying yet challenging endeavour. To make an informed choice that aligns with your cooking preferences and lifestyle, consider the following factors as you embark on your air fryer selection journey.

Capacity and Size

Begin by assessing how much food you typically prepare. Air fryers come in various sizes, usually measured in quarts. A smaller air fryer is ideal for individuals or couples, while larger families may opt for models with a higher capacity. Also, consider the physical dimensions of the air fryer to ensure it fits comfortably in your kitchen space.

Wattage and Cooking Power

Wattage directly impacts an air fryer's cooking speed and efficiency. Higher wattage often translates to quicker cooking times. However, be mindful of your kitchen's electrical capacity, as higher wattage models may require more power.

Temperature and Cooking Settings

Look for an air fryer with a wide temperature range, typically spanning from around 180°F to 400°F (80°C to 200°C). This versatility allows you to prepare a variety of dishes. Additionally, multiple cooking presets—such as for roasting, baking, and grilling—can simplify the cooking process and enhance your culinary repertoire.

User-Friendly Controls

An intuitive control panel makes your cooking experience smoother. Digital interfaces with touch controls and clear displays offer precise settings. Some models even come with pre-programmed cooking times and temperatures for common dishes.

Additional Features

Certain air fryers come equipped with extra functionalities

like rotisserie options, dehydrators, and even toaster oven capabilities. Evaluate your cooking needs and assess whether these additional features align with your culinary aspirations.

Build Quality and Durability
Invest in an air fryer made from sturdy materials. Stainless steel and high-quality plastics are excellent choices as they enhance longevity. A well-built air fryer will withstand regular use and serve you well for years to come.

Reviews and Reputation
Reading reviews from other users can provide valuable insights into the actual performance of the air fryer. Look for user feedback on cooking results, ease of use, and overall satisfaction.

Price Consideration
Air fryers come in a range of price points. While more expensive models might offer additional features and higher build quality, budget-friendly options can still deliver excellent results. Set a budget that aligns with your needs and explore models within that range.

Warranty and Customer Support
Check the manufacturer's warranty to ensure that you're covered in case of any malfunctions or defects. Good customer support can be invaluable if you encounter any issues with your air fryer.

Brand Reputation
Opt for reputable brands known for producing high-quality kitchen appliances. Well-established brands often provide better reliability, customer support, and product consistency.

Kitchen Aesthetic
Lastly, consider the aesthetics of the air fryer. Since it will likely be a countertop fixture, choose a design that complements your kitchen's decor.

Remember, the perfect air fryer for you is the one that aligns with your cooking style, kitchen space, and preferences. By taking the time to evaluate these factors, you'll be well-equipped to make an informed decision and embark on your culinary journey with the ideal air fryer companion.

Ninja has established itself as a prominent name in the world of kitchen appliances, and their air fryers are no exception. With a focus on innovation, versatility, and quality, Ninja offers a variety of air fryer models that cater to different cooking needs. You can trust that Ninja is selling quality air frying products due to these five air fryers being the top five sellers in the Amazon appliances category! Let's take a closer look at the top-selling models and what makes each one unique.

Ninja Dual Zone Cooker (DZ401) and Ninja Dual Zone Cooker (DZ201)

The Ninja Dual Zone Cookers are exceptional choices for those seeking advanced cooking capabilities. They feature two independent cooking zones, each with its own temperature and fan settings. This innovation allows you to simultaneously cook two different dishes with precision, ensuring that flavours and textures are perfectly preserved. From appetisers to main courses, the Dual Zone Cookers open up a world of culinary possibilities.

Ninja Air Fryer Max XL (AF161)

The Ninja Air Fryer Max XL boasts a spacious cooking basket, making it an ideal option for families or larger gatherings. With a 5.5-quart capacity, it can accommodate generous portions of your favourite dishes. Its powerful performance ensures even cooking and satisfying crunch, making it a favourite for those who love to entertain.

Ninja Foodi Digital Air Fry Oven (FT102CO)

The Ninja Foodi Digital Air Fry Oven takes the air frying experience to a new level. This model combines air frying technology with the versatility of a traditional oven. With features like adjustable temperature, multiple cooking functions, and a digital display, it's perfect for those who want an all-in-one appliance that can roast, bake, and air fry with precision.

Ninja Air Fryer (AF101)

The Ninja Air Fryer (AF101) is a fantastic entry-level model that doesn't compromise on quality. With a compact design and straightforward controls, it's an excellent choice for those new to air frying. It offers a convenient way to enjoy healthier versions of your favourite fried foods without overwhelming features.

Ninja Foodi 10-in-1 XL Pro Air Fry Oven (DT251)

The Ninja Foodi 10-in-1 XL Pro Air Fry Oven is a true kitchen powerhouse. With its 10 cooking functions, including air frying, toasting, and dehydrating, it's like having a versatile cooking assistant at your fingertips. The XL capacity ensures you can prepare larger meals or multiple dishes in a single batch.

How to Use Ninja Air Fryers: A Step-by-Step Guide

Using a Ninja air fryer is a straightforward process that yields delicious and healthy results. Here's a step-by-step guide to get you started:

Step 1: Preheat the Air Fryer:
Place your Ninja air fryer on a stable surface and plug it in. Set the desired temperature and preheat the air fryer for a few minutes. Now is also when you should choose your desired function for example roast or broil.

Step 2: Prepare the Food:
While the air fryer is preheating, prepare your ingredients. Lightly coat the food with a small amount of oil if desired, as this can enhance the crispiness of the final result.

Step 3: Load the Basket:
Open the air fryer basket and place your prepared food inside. Make sure not to overcrowd the basket,

allowing proper air circulation for even cooking.

Step 4: Set the Time and Temperature:
Close the basket and set the cooking time and temperature using the control panel. Follow the recipe's recommended settings or your personal preferences.

Step 5: Start Cooking:
Press the start button to initiate the cooking process. The air fryer's powerful fan and heating element will work together to circulate hot air around the food, creating a crispy exterior.

Step 6: Check and Shake:
Depending on the recipe, you may need to pause the cooking process and shake the basket to ensure even cooking. Some models have a reminder feature that alerts you to shake the basket at a certain point.

Step 7: Monitor and Serve:
Keep an eye on the cooking progress through the air fryer's transparent lid or window. When the food reaches the desired level of crispiness and doneness, carefully remove the basket and serve your culinary creation.

Step 8: Cleaning and Storage:
After the air fryer has cooled down, clean the basket, tray, and any removable parts. Many parts are dishwasher-safe, making cleanup a breeze. Store the air fryer in a cool, dry place for future use.

With these simple steps, you're well on your way to mastering the art of air frying with your Ninja air fryer. Experiment with various recipes and ingredients to unlock the full potential of this versatile kitchen tool.

Tips and Tricks for Using the Ninja Dual Zone Air Fryer

The Ninja Dual Zone Air Fryer, with its unique dual cooking zones, offers a realm of possibilities for creating culinary masterpieces. To make the most of this advanced kitchen appliance, consider these tips and tricks that will elevate your cooking experience and allow you to harness the full potential of its innovative design.

Embrace Simultaneous Cooking
The hallmark feature of the Ninja Dual Zone Air Fryer is its ability to cook two different dishes simultaneously with independent settings for temperature and fan speed. Utilise this capability to its fullest by pairing foods that have similar cooking

times. Imagine preparing crispy fries on one side while air frying chicken tenders on the other—both perfectly cooked, without cross-flavoring.

Maintain Food Separation
While the Dual Zone Air Fryer allows cooking multiple dishes at once, it's essential to maintain some separation between them. Use the included air fryer divider to create a barrier between the two zones, preventing flavours from mingling while ensuring even cooking results.

Optimise Temperature and Time Settings
Since each zone can be adjusted independently, you have the flexibility to experiment with different temperature and time settings for each dish. Keep in mind that certain foods may release moisture during cooking, affecting the overall cooking environment. Adjust the settings accordingly to achieve your desired results.

Utilise the Broil Feature
The Dual Zone Air Fryer offers a broil feature that's perfect for adding a finishing touch to dishes. Use it to brown the tops of casseroles, melt cheese, or achieve a delightful caramelization on desserts.

Preheat for Consistency
Just like with any air fryer, preheating the Dual Zone Air Fryer is essential for consistent cooking results. Preheating ensures that the cooking chambers are at the desired temperature from the start, contributing to even and efficient cooking.

Experiment with Different Cuisines
The Dual Zone Air Fryer's versatility is a boon for experimenting with global cuisines. Imagine preparing a batch of appetising spring rolls in one zone while crafting a flavorful Mediterranean-inspired dish in the other—diversifying your culinary repertoire has never been easier.

Mindful Menu Planning
When planning your meals, consider the types of dishes you want to prepare together. Certain ingredients might release strong aromas that could affect the flavours of neighbouring dishes. Opt for complementary flavours or adjust the timing to accommodate different cooking stages.

Rotate and Swap
During cooking, occasionally swap the positions of the dishes or rotate them within their zones. This helps ensure uniform cooking and browning, particularly

if you're cooking dishes that have varying shapes or sizes.

Monitor and Adjust

Regularly monitor the cooking progress of each dish. As you become familiar with your Dual Zone Air Fryer, you'll develop an intuition for when to adjust settings, rotate dishes, or even swap their positions for optimal results.

Embrace Creativity

The Dual Zone Air Fryer's innovation encourages culinary creativity. Feel free to devise your own cooking combinations and techniques, pushing the boundaries of what's possible with this remarkable appliance.

By incorporating these tips and tricks into your culinary endeavours, you'll be able to unlock the full potential of the Ninja Dual Zone Air Fryer and create dishes that not only tantalise your taste buds but also showcase the impressive capabilities of this advanced kitchen tool.

Cleaning and Maintenance

Maintaining the cleanliness and functionality of your Ninja air fryer is essential to ensure that it continues to deliver outstanding cooking results. Here's a guide to help you effectively clean and maintain your air fryer, keeping it in prime condition for countless delicious meals.

Cool Down Before Cleaning

Always allow your air fryer to cool down after use before you begin the cleaning process. This not only prevents accidental burns but also makes it easier to handle the components.

Unplug and Disassemble

Before you start cleaning, make sure the air fryer is unplugged from the power source. Next, disassemble the components that can be removed, such as the cooking basket, tray, and any additional attachments.

Hand Wash Removable Parts

Most removable parts, such as the cooking basket and tray, can be hand-washed with warm, soapy water. Use a non-abrasive sponge or cloth to gently scrub away any food residue. Rinse thoroughly and allow the parts to air dry before reassembly.

Check for Dishwasher Compatibility

Refer to your air fryer's manual to determine which parts are dishwasher-safe. Many modern air fryers come with dishwasher-safe components, making cleanup even more convenient. Place these parts on the top rack of your dishwasher for a hassle-free cleaning experience.

Clean the Interior and Exterior

Wipe down the interior of the air fryer with a damp cloth to remove any food particles or grease. For the exterior, use a mild detergent and a soft cloth to wipe away any fingerprints, stains, or splatters. Avoid using abrasive cleaners that might damage the surface.

Address Tough Stains

For stubborn stains or residue, create a paste using baking soda and water. Apply the paste to the affected area, let it sit for a few minutes, and then gently scrub with a soft cloth. Rinse thoroughly and dry.

Clean the Heating Element

Regularly check the heating element of your air fryer for any buildup of grease or food particles. If necessary, use a soft brush or cloth to gently remove debris. Ensure the heating element is completely dry before using the air fryer again.

Avoid Submerging Electrical Components

Never submerge the main unit or any electrical components in water. These parts should be wiped down with a damp cloth, ensuring that no water enters the internal components.

Regular Maintenance

Periodically, inspect the air fryer for any signs of wear, damage, or malfunction. This includes checking the power cord, plug, and control panel. If you notice anything unusual, contact the manufacturer or a qualified technician for assistance.

Store Properly

When not in use, store your air fryer in a cool, dry place. Make sure all components are completely dry before reassembly and storage to prevent the growth of mould or bacteria.

By following these cleaning and maintenance practices, you can ensure that your Ninja air fryer remains not only a reliable kitchen companion but also a hygienic and safe appliance for all your cooking adventures. Regular upkeep will help extend the lifespan of your air fryer and guarantee consistent, flavorful results with each use.

Chapter 3: Breakfast

Crispy Breakfast Burritos

Serves: 4
Prep time: 15 minutes / Cook time: 10 minutes

Ingredients:

- 200g cooked and crumbled breakfast sausages
- 100g shredded cheddar cheese
- 4 large eggs, beaten
- 60ml whole milk
- 1/4 tsp garlic powder
- 1/4 tsp onion powder
- Salt and black pepper, to taste
- 4 medium flour tortillas
- Cooking oil spray

Preparation instructions:

1. In a bowl, combine the cooked breakfast sausages and shredded cheddar cheese.
2. In another bowl, whisk together the beaten eggs, whole milk, garlic powder, onion powder, salt, and black pepper.
3. Heat a non-stick skillet over medium heat and scramble the egg mixture until cooked through.
4. Lay out the flour tortillas and divide the scrambled eggs and sausage-cheese mixture among them.
5. Roll each tortilla into a burrito, tucking in the sides as you go.
6. Preheat the Air Fryer to 180°C for 5 minutes.
7. Lightly spray the burritos with cooking oil and air fry at 180°C for about 10 minutes, or until they're crispy and golden.
8. Serve hot and enjoy!

Blueberry Lemon Pancake Bites

Serves: 4
Prep time: 10 minutes / Cook time: 8 minutes

Ingredients:

- 150g pancake mix
- 120ml milk
- Zest of 1 lemon
- 100g fresh blueberries
- Icing sugar, for dusting

Preparation instructions:

1. In a bowl, whisk together the pancake mix, milk, and lemon zest until just combined.
2. Gently fold in the fresh blueberries.
3. Preheat the Air Fryer to 180°C for 5 minutes.
4. Lightly grease the air fryer basket with oil or use liners.
5. Spoon the pancake batter into the wells of the air fryer basket, filling each about 2/3 full.
6. Air fry at 180°C for about 8 minutes, or until the pancake bites are cooked through and golden on the outside.
7. Dust with icing sugar and serve warm.

Veggie-Packed Omelette Muffins

Serves: 4
Prep time: 15 minutes / Cook time: 12 minutes

Ingredients:

- 6 large eggs
- 80ml milk
- Salt and black pepper, to taste
- 50g chopped peppers
- 50g chopped spinach
- 50g diced tomatoes
- 50g diced onions
- 50g shredded cheddar cheese

Preparation instructions:

1. In a bowl, whisk together the eggs, milk, salt, and black pepper.
2. Stir in the chopped peppers, spinach, tomatoes, onions, and shredded cheddar cheese.
3. Preheat the Air Fryer to 180°C for 5 minutes.
4. Grease silicone muffin cups or use liners.
5. Pour the egg and veggie mixture into the muffin cups, filling each about 2/3 full.
6. Air fry at 180°C for about 12 minutes, or until

the omelette muffins are puffed up and cooked through.

7. Let cool slightly before removing from the muffin cups and serving.

Cinnamon Sugar French Toast Sticks

Serves: 4
Prep time: 10 minutes / Cook time: 6 minutes

Ingredients:
- 8 slices of bread, cut into sticks
- 2 large eggs
- 80ml milk
- 1 tsp vanilla extract
- 1 tsp ground cinnamon
- 1 tbsp granulated sugar
- Cooking oil spray

Preparation instructions:
1. In a bowl, whisk together the eggs, milk, vanilla extract, ground cinnamon, and granulated sugar.
2. Preheat the Air Fryer to 180°C for 5 minutes.
3. Dip each breadstick into the egg mixture, allowing excess to drip off.
4. Lightly grease the air fryer basket with cooking oil spray.
5. Place the coated bread sticks in a single layer in the air fryer basket, leaving space between them.
6. Air fry at 180°C for about 6 minutes, turning the sticks halfway through, until they are golden and crispy.
7. Serve the French toast sticks with your favourite syrup or dipping sauce.

Sausage and Cheese Breakfast Pockets

Serves: 4
Prep time: 15 minutes / Cook time: 12 minutes

Ingredients:
- 200g puff pastry, thawed
- 8 cooked breakfast sausages, sliced
- 100g shredded cheddar cheese
- 1 large egg, beaten
- Cooking oil spray

Preparation instructions:
1. Preheat the Air Fryer to 180°C for 5 minutes.
2. Roll out the puff pastry and cut it into 4 equal squares.
3. On each square, place a few slices of cooked breakfast sausage and a sprinkle of shredded cheddar cheese.
4. Fold the puff pastry over the filling to form a triangle and press the edges to seal.
5. Lightly grease the air fryer basket with cooking oil spray.
6. Brush the tops of the pastry pockets with the beaten egg.
7. Place the pockets in the air fryer basket and air fry at 180°C for about 12 minutes, or until the pockets are golden brown and puffed up.
8. Let cool slightly before serving.

Hash Brown Waffles with Bacon

Serves: 4
Prep time: 15 minutes / Cook time: 10 minutes

Ingredients:
- 400g shredded hash brown potatoes
- 100g cooked bacon, crumbled
- 1/2 tsp onion powder
- Salt and black pepper, to taste
- Cooking oil spray

Preparation instructions:
1. In a bowl, combine the shredded hash brown potatoes, crumbled cooked bacon, onion powder, salt, and black pepper.
2. Preheat the Air Fryer to 190°C for 5 minutes.
3. Lightly grease the waffle plates of the air fryer with cooking oil spray.
4. Place a portion of the hash brown mixture onto the waffle plates, spreading it out evenly.
5. Close the air fryer and cook at 190°C for about 10 minutes, or until the hash browns are crispy and golden.

6. Carefully remove the hash brown waffle and serve warm.

Banana Nut Air-Fried Muffins

Serves: 4
Prep time: 15 minutes / Cook time: 20 minutes

Ingredients:
- 150g all-purpose flour
- 1 tsp baking powder
- 1/2 tsp baking soda
- 1/4 tsp ground cinnamon
- 1/4 tsp salt
- 2 ripe bananas, mashed
- 80 ml vegetable oil
- 80g granulated sugar
- 1 large egg
- 60ml buttermilk
- 50g chopped walnuts

Preparation instructions:
1. In a bowl, whisk together the all-purpose flour, baking powder, baking soda, ground cinnamon, and salt.
2. In another bowl, combine the mashed bananas, vegetable oil, granulated sugar, egg, and buttermilk.
3. Gradually add the dry Ingredients to the wet Ingredients, mixing until just combined.
4. Fold in the chopped walnuts.
5. Preheat the Air Fryer to 160°C for 5 minutes.
6. Grease silicone muffin cups or use liners.
7. Divide the muffin batter evenly among the cups.
8. Place the muffin cups in the air fryer basket and air fry at 160°C for about 20 minutes, or until a toothpick inserted into the centre of a muffin comes out clean.
9. Let the muffins cool slightly before serving.

Spinach and Feta Breakfast Quesadillas

Serves: 4
Prep time: 15 minutes / Cook time: 8 minutes

Ingredients:
- 4 large whole wheat tortillas
- 150g fresh spinach, chopped
- 100g crumbled feta cheese
- 4 large eggs, beaten
- Salt and black pepper, to taste
- Cooking oil spray

Preparation instructions:
1. Preheat the Air Fryer to 180°C for 5 minutes.
2. In a bowl, combine the chopped fresh spinach and crumbled feta cheese.
3. Heat a non-stick skillet over medium heat and scramble the beaten eggs until cooked through.
4. Lay out the whole wheat tortillas and divide the scrambled eggs and spinach-feta mixture among them.
5. Fold each tortilla in half to form a quesadilla.
6. Lightly grease the air fryer basket with cooking oil spray.
7. Place the quesadillas in the basket and air fry at 180°C for about 8 minutes, or until they're heated through and crispy on the outside.
8. Serve the quesadillas warm.

Apple Cinnamon Breakfast Pastries

Serves: 4
Prep time: 15 minutes / Cook time: 12 minutes

Ingredients:
- 1 sheet puff pastry, thawed
- 2 medium apples, peeled, cored, and diced
- 2 tbsp granulated sugar
- 1/2 tsp ground cinnamon
- 1/4 tsp ground nutmeg
- 1/4 tsp vanilla extract
- 1 large egg, beaten
- Icing sugar, for dusting

Preparation instructions:
1. Preheat the Air Fryer to 180°C for 5 minutes.
2. In a bowl, mix together the diced apples, granulated sugar, ground cinnamon, ground nutmeg, and vanilla extract.

3. Roll out the puff pastry and cut it into 4 equal squares.
4. Place a portion of the apple mixture onto the centre of each puff pastry square.
5. Fold the corners of the puff pastry over the apple mixture to create a triangular shape.
6. Press the edges to seal the pastries.
7. Lightly brush the tops of the pastries with the beaten egg.
8. Place the pastries in the air fryer basket and air fry at 180°C for about 12 minutes, or until the pastries are puffed up and golden brown.
9. Dust with icing sugar before serving.

Greek Yoghurt Parfait Delight

Serves: 4
Prep time: 10 minutes

Ingredients:
- 400g Greek yoghurt
- 100g granola
- 200g mixed berries (strawberries, blueberries, raspberries)
- 2 tbsp honey
- 1 tsp vanilla extract

Preparation instructions:
1. In a bowl, mix together the Greek yoghurt, honey, and vanilla extract.
2. Preheat the Air Fryer to 180°C for 5 minutes.
3. Layer the Greek yoghurt mixture, granola, and mixed berries in serving glasses or bowls.
4. Place the glasses or bowls in the air fryer basket and air fry at 180°C for about 3 minutes, just to warm up the layers slightly.
5. Serve the parfait warm or chilled, as desired.

Cheddar and Chive Breakfast Biscuits

Serves: 4
Prep time: 15 minutes / Cook time: 12 minutes

Ingredients:
- 250g self-raising flour
- 1/2 tsp baking powder
- 1/4 tsp salt
- 100g shredded cheddar cheese
- 2 tbsp chopped fresh chives
- 120ml whole milk
- 60g unsalted butter, melted
- 1 large egg, beaten

Preparation instructions:
1. Preheat the Air Fryer to 180°C for 5 minutes.
2. In a bowl, mix together the self-raising flour, baking powder, and salt.
3. Stir in the shredded cheddar cheese and chopped fresh chives.
4. In another bowl, whisk together the whole milk, melted butter, and beaten egg.
5. Add the wet Ingredients to the dry Ingredients and mix until just combined.
6. Divide the dough into 4 equal portions and shape each into a biscuit.
7. Lightly grease the air fryer basket with cooking oil spray.
8. Place the biscuits in the basket and air fry at 180°C for about 12 minutes, or until they're golden brown and cooked through.
9. Let the biscuits cool slightly before serving.

Mixed Berry Breakfast Bars

Serves: 4
Prep time: 15 minutes / Cook time: 25 minutes

Ingredients:
- 150g oats
- 50g whole wheat flour
- 50g brown sugar
- 1/2 tsp baking powder
- 1/4 tsp ground cinnamon
- Pinch of salt
- 80 ml vegetable oil
- 80 ml honey
- 1 large egg
- 100g mixed berries (blueberries, raspberries, strawberries)

Preparation instructions:

1. Preheat the Air Fryer to 160°C for 5 minutes.
2. In a bowl, mix together the oats, whole wheat flour, brown sugar, baking powder, ground cinnamon, and salt.
3. In another bowl, whisk together the vegetable oil, honey, and egg until well combined.
4. Combine the wet and dry Ingredients, mixing until a dough forms.
5. Gently fold in the mixed berries.
6. Press the mixture into a baking dish that fits in your air fryer.
7. Place the baking dish in the air fryer basket and air fry at 160°C for about 25 minutes, or until the bars are golden brown and set.
8. Allow the bars to cool before cutting into squares.

Breakfast Sausage Links with Maple Glaze

Serves: 4
Prep time: 5 minutes / Cook time: 12 minutes

Ingredients:
- 8 cooked breakfast sausage links
- 60ml maple syrup
- 1 tbsp Dijon mustard
- 1/2 tsp apple cider vinegar

Preparation instructions:

1. Preheat the Air Fryer to 180°C for 5 minutes.
2. In a bowl, whisk together the maple syrup, Dijon mustard, and apple cider vinegar to make the glaze.
3. Place the cooked breakfast sausage links in the air fryer basket.
4. Brush the sausage links with the maple glaze.
5. Air fry at 180°C for about 12 minutes, brushing with additional glaze halfway through, until the sausages are heated through and the glaze is caramelised.
6. Serve the sausage links warm.

Ham and Egg Breakfast Tacos

Serves: 4
Prep time: 10 minutes / Cook time: 8 minutes

Ingredients:
- 8 small corn tortillas
- 8 slices cooked ham
- 4 large eggs
- Salt and black pepper, to taste
- Chopped fresh parsley, for garnish

Preparation instructions:

1. Preheat the Air Fryer to 180°C for 5 minutes.
2. Place the corn tortillas in the air fryer basket and air fry at 180°C for about 2 minutes, until they're warm and slightly crispy.
3. Lay a slice of cooked ham in each tortilla.
4. Crack an egg into a small bowl, then carefully slide it onto the ham in each tortilla.
5. Season the eggs with salt and black pepper.
6. Air fry at 180°C for about 6 minutes, or until the egg whites are set but the yolks are still slightly runny.
7. Garnish with chopped fresh parsley before serving.

Avocado and Egg Breakfast Pitas

Serves: 4
Prep time: 10 minutes / Cook time: 8 minutes

Ingredients:
- 2 ripe avocados, sliced
- 4 whole wheat pitas
- 4 large eggs
- Salt and black pepper, to taste
- Chopped fresh coriander, for garnish

Preparation instructions:

1. Preheat the Air Fryer to 180°C for 5 minutes.
2. Cut a small pocket in each pita to hold the Ingredients.
3. Place the pitas in the air fryer basket and air fry at 180°C for about 2 minutes, until they're warm and slightly crispy.

4. While the pitas are warming, crack an egg into a small bowl, then carefully slide it into the pocket of each pita.
5. Arrange avocado slices around the egg in each pita.
6. Season with salt and black pepper.
7. Air fry at 180°C for about 6 minutes, or until the egg whites are set but the yolks are still slightly runny.
8. Garnish with chopped fresh coriander before serving.

Peanut Butter Banana Toast Crunch

Serves: 4
Prep time: 5 minutes / Cook time: 5 minutes

Ingredients:
- 4 slices whole wheat bread
- 4 tbsp peanut butter
- 2 ripe bananas, sliced
- 4 tbsp granola
- Honey, for drizzling

Preparation instructions:
1. Preheat the Air Fryer to 180°C for 5 minutes.
2. Lightly toast the whole wheat bread slices.
3. Spread 1 tablespoon of peanut butter on each slice of toasted bread.
4. Arrange banana slices on top of the peanut butter.
5. Sprinkle granola over the bananas.
6. Place the prepared toasts in the air fryer basket and air fry at 180°C for about 5 minutes, until the granola is golden and crispy.
7. Drizzle with honey before serving.

Breakfast Potato Hash with Peppers

Serves: 4
Prep time: 10 minutes / Cook time: 15 minutes

Ingredients:
- 400g diced potatoes
- 1 red pepper, diced
- 1 green pepper, diced
- 1 onion, diced
- 2 tbsp olive oil
- 1/2 tsp garlic powder
- 1/2 tsp paprika
- Salt and black pepper, to taste
- Chopped fresh parsley, for garnish

Preparation instructions:
1. Preheat the Air Fryer to 200°C for 5 minutes.
2. In a bowl, toss together the diced potatoes, diced peppers, diced onion, olive oil, garlic powder, paprika, salt, and black pepper.
3. Place the potato mixture in the air fryer basket.
4. Air fry at 200°C for about 15 minutes, shaking the basket or stirring halfway through, until the potatoes are golden and crispy.
5. Garnish with chopped fresh parsley before serving.

Chocolate Protein Waffles

Serves: 4
Prep time: 15 minutes / Cook time: 10 minutes

Ingredients:
- 180g whole wheat flour
- 30g cocoa powder
- 1 scoop chocolate protein powder
- 1 tbsp baking powder
- 1/4 tsp salt
- 2 large eggs
- 240 ml milk
- 2 tbsp honey
- 2 tbsp Greek yoghurt
- Cooking oil spray

Preparation instructions:
1. Preheat the Air Fryer to 180°C for 5 minutes.
2. In a bowl, whisk together the whole wheat flour, cocoa powder, chocolate protein powder, baking powder, and salt.
3. In another bowl, whisk together the eggs, milk, honey, and Greek yoghurt.
4. Combine the wet and dry Ingredients, mixing

until just combined.

5. Lightly grease the waffle plates of the air fryer with cooking oil spray.
6. Spoon the batter onto the waffle plates, spreading it out evenly.
7. Close the air fryer and cook at 180°C for about 10 minutes, or until the waffles are cooked through and crispy.
8. Serve the chocolate protein waffles warm.

Raspberry Almond Danish Swirls

Serves: 4
Prep time: 15 minutes / Cook time: 12 minutes

Ingredients:
* 1 sheet puff pastry, thawed
* 100g raspberry jam
* 50g almond flakes
* 1 large egg, beaten
* Icing sugar, for dusting

Preparation instructions:
1. Preheat the Air Fryer to 180°C for 5 minutes.
2. Roll out the puff pastry and cut it into 4 equal squares.
3. Spread raspberry jam on each puff pastry square, leaving a border around the edges.
4. Sprinkle almond flakes over the jam.
5. Roll up each puff pastry square from one side to form a swirl.
6. Lightly brush the tops of the swirls with the beaten egg.
7. Place the swirls in the air fryer basket and air fry at 180°C for about 12 minutes, or until they're golden brown and puffed up.
8. Dust with icing sugar before serving.

Overnight Oats Crunchy Clusters

Serves: 4
Prep time: 10 minutes / Rest time: Overnight

Ingredients:
* 200g rolled oats
* 80ml milk
* 80ml Greek yoghurt
* 2 tbsp honey
* 1/2 tsp vanilla extract
* 50g chopped nuts (e.g., almonds, walnuts)
* 50g dried cranberries or raisins

Preparation instructions:
1. In a bowl, mix together the rolled oats, milk, Greek yoghurt, honey, and vanilla extract.
2. Stir in the chopped nuts and dried cranberries or raisins.
3. Cover the bowl and refrigerate the mixture overnight to allow the oats to soak and thicken.
4. Preheat the Air Fryer to 160°C for 5 minutes.
5. Spread the oat mixture evenly on the air fryer basket.
6. Air fry at 160°C for about 8 minutes, shaking the basket or stirring the oats occasionally, until the clusters are golden and crispy.
7. Allow the clusters to cool before breaking them into smaller pieces.

Breakfast Potatoes

Serves: 4
Prep time: 5 mins / Cook time: 20 mins

Ingredients:
* 500g potatoes, peeled and diced into 1 cm cubes
* 2 tbsp olive oil
* 1 tsp paprika
* 1 tsp garlic powder
* Salt and pepper, to taste

Preparation instructions:
1. Preparation Instructions:
2. Preheat your air fryer to 200C.
3. In a large bowl, mix together the potatoes, olive oil, paprika, garlic powder, salt, and pepper.
4. Place the mixture in the air fryer basket and cook for 20-25 minutes, or until the potatoes are crispy and tender.

Breakfast Burrito

Serves: 2

Prep time: 5 mins / Cook time: 5- 7 mins

Ingredients:

- 4 small flour tortillas
- 100 g scrambled eggs
- 60 g black beans, drained and rinsed
- 75 g diced tomato
- 60 g diced avocado
- 25 g shredded cheese
- Hot sauce, optional
- Preparation Instructions:

Preparation instructions:

1. Preheat your air fryer to 180C.
2. Lay out the tortillas on a flat surface.
3. Divide the eggs, black beans, tomato, avocado, and cheese evenly among the tortillas.
4. Roll the tortillas up tightly and place them seam-side down in the air fryer basket.
5. Cook for 5-7 minutes until the burritos are heated through and the edges are crispy.
6. Serve with hot sauce, if desired.

Cheddar Eggs

Serves 2

Prep time: 5 minutes / Cook time: 15 minutes

- 4 large eggs
- 2 tablespoons unsalted butter, melted
- 120 ml shredded sharp Cheddar cheese

Preparation instructions:

1. Crack eggs into a round baking dish and whisk. Place dish into the air fryer basket.
2. Adjust the temperature to 204°C and set the timer for 10 minutes.

3. After 5 minutes, stir the eggs and add the butter and cheese. Let cook 3 more minutes and stir again.
4. Allow eggs to finish cooking an additional 2 minutes or remove if they are to your desired liking.
5. Use a fork to fluff. Serve warm

Scotch Eggs

Serves 4

Prep time: 10 minutes / Cook time: 20 to 25 minutes

2 tablespoons flour, plus extra for coating

450 g sausage meat

4 hard-boiled eggs, peeled

1 raw egg

1 tablespoon water

Oil for misting or cooking spray

Crumb Coating:

180 ml panko bread crumbs

180 ml flour

Preparation instructions:

1. Combine flour with sausage meat and mix thoroughly.
2. Divide into 4 equal portions and mold each around a hard-boiled egg so the sausage completely covers the egg.
3. In a small bowl, beat together the raw egg and water.
4. Dip sausage-covered eggs in the remaining flour, then the egg mixture, then roll in the crumb coating.
5. Air fry at 182°C for 10 minutes. Spray eggs, turn, and spray other side.
6. Continue cooking for another 10 to 15 minutes or until sausage is well done.

Chapter 4: Main Courses (Family Favourites)

Classic Air-Fried Chicken Tenders

Serves: 4
Prep time: 15 minutes / Cook time: 15 minutes

Ingredients:
- 400g chicken tenders
- 80g breadcrumbs
- 40g grated Parmesan cheese
- 1/2 tsp paprika
- 1/2 tsp garlic powder
- 1/4 tsp salt
- 1/4 tsp black pepper
- 1 large egg
- Cooking oil spray

Preparation instructions:
1. Preheat the Air Fryer to 190°C for 5 minutes.
2. In a bowl, mix together the breadcrumbs, grated Parmesan cheese, paprika, garlic powder, salt, and black pepper.
3. Beat the egg in a separate bowl.
4. Dip each chicken tender into the beaten egg, then coat with the breadcrumb mixture.
5. Lightly grease the air fryer basket with cooking oil spray.
6. Place the coated chicken tenders in the basket in a single layer.
7. Air fry at 190°C for about 15 minutes, flipping the tenders halfway through, until they're crispy and cooked through.
8. Serve the chicken tenders with your favourite dipping sauce.

Cheesy Beef and Veggie Stuffed peppers

Serves: 4
Prep time: 20 minutes / Cook time: 20 minutes

Ingredients:
- 4 large peppers, halved and seeds removed
- 300g minced beef
- 1 onion, finely chopped
- 1 carrot, finely chopped
- 1 courgette, finely chopped
- 200g cooked rice
- 150g shredded cheddar cheese
- 1 tsp Italian seasoning
- Salt and black pepper, to taste

Preparation instructions:
1. Preheat the Air Fryer to 180°C for 5 minutes.
2. In a skillet, cook the minced beef until browned. Remove excess fat.
3. Add the chopped onion, carrot, and courgette to the skillet. Cook until vegetables are tender.
4. Stir in the cooked rice, shredded cheddar cheese, Italian seasoning, salt, and black pepper.
5. Stuff each pepper half with the beef and veggie mixture.
6. Place the stuffed peppers in the air fryer basket.
7. Air fry at 180°C for about 20 minutes, or until the peppers are tender and the cheese is melted and bubbly.
8. Serve the cheesy beef and veggie stuffed peppers.

Creamy Garlic Parmesan Pasta

Serves: 4
Prep time: 10 minutes / Cook time: 10 minutes

Ingredients:
- 300g pasta (spaghetti, fettuccine, or your choice)
- 60ml heavy cream
- 50g grated Parmesan cheese
- 2 cloves garlic, minced
- 2 tbsp unsalted butter
- Salt and black pepper, to taste
- Chopped fresh parsley, for garnish

Preparation instructions:
1. Cook the pasta according to the package instructions until al dente. Drain and set aside.
2. Preheat the Air Fryer to 180°C for 5 minutes.
3. In a bowl, mix together the heavy cream, grated Parmesan cheese, minced garlic, and unsalted butter.
4. Place the cooked pasta in the air fryer basket.
5. Pour the creamy mixture over the pasta.
6. Air fry at 180°C for about 10 minutes, stirring occasionally, until the sauce is heated through and creamy.
7. Season with salt and black pepper to taste.
8. Garnish with chopped fresh parsley before serving.

BBQ Pulled Pork Sliders

Serves: 4
Prep time: 15 minutes / Cook time: 20 minutes

Ingredients:
- 400g cooked pulled pork
- 8 mini slider buns
- 120ml barbecue sauce
- 1/2 red onion, thinly sliced
- Coleslaw, for topping (optional)

Preparation instructions:
1. Preheat the Air Fryer to 180°C for 5 minutes.
2. In a bowl, mix the pulled pork with barbecue sauce.
3. Place the pulled pork mixture in the air fryer basket.
4. Air fry at 180°C for about 10 minutes, stirring occasionally, until the pork is heated through.
5. Slice the mini slider buns and toast them in the air fryer for a minute or two.
6. Assemble the sliders by placing a portion of pulled pork on the bottom bun, topping with red onion slices and coleslaw if desired, and covering with the top bun.
7. Serve the BBQ pulled pork sliders.

Crispy Coconut Shrimp

Serves: 4
Prep time: 20 minutes / Cook time: 10 minutes

Ingredients:
- 400g large shrimp, peeled and deveined
- 80g shredded coconut
- 60g breadcrumbs
- 2 large eggs, beaten
- 1/2 tsp garlic powder
- 1/2 tsp paprika
- Salt and black pepper, to taste
- Cooking oil spray

Preparation instructions:
1. Preheat the Air Fryer to 180°C for 5 minutes.
2. In a bowl, mix together the shredded coconut, breadcrumbs, garlic powder, paprika, salt, and black pepper.
3. Dip each shrimp into the beaten eggs, then coat with the coconut-breadcrumb mixture.
4. Lightly grease the air fryer basket with cooking oil spray.
5. Place the coated shrimp in the basket in a single layer.
6. Air fry at 180°C for about 10 minutes, flipping the shrimp halfway through, until they're golden and crispy.
7. Serve the crispy coconut shrimp with your favourite dipping sauce.

Italian Herb Chicken Drumsticks

Serves: 4
Prep time: 15 minutes / Cook time: 25 minutes

Ingredients:
- 8 chicken drumsticks
- 2 tbsp olive oil
- 2 tsp Italian seasoning
- 1/2 tsp garlic powder
- 1/2 tsp onion powder
- Salt and black pepper, to taste
- Chopped fresh parsley, for garnish

Preparation instructions:

1. Preheat the Air Fryer to 190°C for 5 minutes.
2. In a bowl, mix together the olive oil, Italian seasoning, garlic powder, onion powder, salt, and black pepper.
3. Rub the mixture over the chicken drumsticks to coat them evenly.
4. Place the chicken drumsticks in the air fryer basket.
5. Air fry at 190°C for about 25 minutes, turning the drumsticks halfway through, until they're cooked through and the skin is crispy.
6. Garnish with chopped fresh parsley before serving.

Teriyaki Glazed Salmon Fillets

Serves: 4
Prep time: 10 minutes / Cook time: 10 minutes

Ingredients:

* 4 salmon fillets
* 80ml teriyaki sauce
* 2 tbsp honey
* 1 tbsp soy sauce
* 1 tsp grated ginger
* 1 tsp minced garlic
* Sesame seeds, for garnish
* Sliced green onions, for garnish

Preparation instructions:

1. Preheat the Air Fryer to 180°C for 5 minutes.
2. In a bowl, whisk together the teriyaki sauce, honey, soy sauce, grated ginger, and minced garlic to make the glaze.
3. Place the salmon fillets in the air fryer basket.
4. Brush the salmon fillets with the teriyaki glaze.
5. Air fry at 180°C for about 10 minutes, basting the fillets with additional glaze halfway through, until the salmon is cooked through and flakes easily.
6. Garnish with sesame seeds and sliced green onions before serving.

Beefy Mushroom Burger Patties

Serves: 4
Prep time: 15 minutes / Cook time: 12 minutes

Ingredients:

* 500g minced beef
* 150g mushrooms, finely chopped
* 1 small onion, finely chopped
* 1 egg
* 2 tbsp breadcrumbs
* 1 tsp Worcestershire sauce
* 1/2 tsp garlic powder
* Salt and black pepper, to taste
* Cooking oil spray

Preparation instructions:

1. Preheat the Air Fryer to 180°C for 5 minutes.
2. In a bowl, mix together the minced beef, chopped mushrooms, chopped onion, egg, breadcrumbs, Worcestershire sauce, garlic powder, salt, and black pepper.
3. Divide the mixture into 4 equal portions and shape each into a burger patty.
4. Lightly grease the air fryer basket with cooking oil spray.
5. Place the burger patties in the basket.
6. Air fry at 180°C for about 12 minutes, flipping the patties halfway through, until they're cooked to your desired level of doneness.
7. Serve the beefy mushroom burger patties on buns with your favourite toppings.

Honey Glazed Chicken Thighs

Serves: 4
Prep time: 10 minutes / Cook time: 20 minutes

Ingredients:

* 8 bone-in, skin-on chicken thighs
* 60ml honey
* 2 tbsp soy sauce
* 1 tbsp Dijon mustard
* 1/2 tsp garlic powder

- Salt and black pepper, to taste

Preparation instructions:
1. Preheat the Air Fryer to 190°C for 5 minutes.
2. In a bowl, whisk together the honey, soy sauce, Dijon mustard, garlic powder, salt, and black pepper to make the glaze.
3. Place the chicken thighs in the air fryer basket, skin side up.
4. Brush the chicken thighs with the honey glaze.
5. Air fry at 190°C for about 20 minutes, basting the thighs with additional glaze halfway through, until the chicken is cooked through and the skin is crispy.
6. Serve the honey glazed chicken thighs.

Spinach and Ricotta Stuffed Shells

Serves: 4
Prep time: 20 minutes / Cook time: 20 minutes

Ingredients:
- 200g jumbo pasta shells
- 200g ricotta cheese
- 100g chopped spinach, cooked and squeezed dry
- 60g grated Parmesan cheese
- 1 egg
- 1/2 tsp dried oregano
- 1/4 tsp garlic powder
- Salt and black pepper, to taste
- 400g marinara sauce

Preparation instructions:
1. Cook the jumbo pasta shells according to package instructions until al dente. Drain and set aside.
2. Preheat the Air Fryer to 180°C for 5 minutes.
3. In a bowl, mix together the ricotta cheese, chopped spinach, grated Parmesan cheese, egg, dried oregano, garlic powder, salt, and black pepper.
4. Stuff each cooked pasta shell with the ricotta and spinach mixture.

5. Place the stuffed shells in the air fryer basket.
6. Air fry at 180°C for about 20 minutes, until the shells are heated through and the edges are slightly crispy.
7. Warm the marinara sauce separately and serve it over the stuffed shells.

Beef and Broccoli Stir-Fry

Serves: 4
Prep time: 15 minutes / Cook time: 10 minutes

Ingredients:
- 300g beef steak, thinly sliced
- 200g broccoli florets
- 1 red pepper, sliced
- 60ml soy sauce
- 2 tbsp oyster sauce
- 1 tbsp sesame oil
- 1 tsp minced ginger
- 2 cloves garlic, minced
- 1 tsp cornstarch
- Cooking oil

Preparation instructions:
1. Preheat the Air Fryer to 200°C for 5 minutes.
2. In a bowl, mix together the soy sauce, oyster sauce, sesame oil, minced ginger, minced garlic, and cornstarch to make the sauce.
3. Preheat a skillet or wok over high heat and add a small amount of cooking oil.
4. Stir-fry the beef slices until browned. Remove from the skillet.
5. Stir-fry the broccoli florets and red pepper until they're tender-crisp.
6. Return the cooked beef to the skillet, pour in the sauce, and stir-fry until the sauce thickens and coats the Ingredients.
7. Preheat the Air Fryer to 180°C for 5 minutes. Place the stir-fry mixture in the air fryer basket.
8. Air fry at 180°C for about 5 minutes to reheat and enhance the flavours.
9. Serve the beef and broccoli stir-fry over steamed rice.

Lemon Herb Roasted Whole Chicken

Serves: 4

Prep time: 15 minutes / Cook time: 1 hour

Ingredients:

- 1 whole chicken (about 1.5 kg)
- 2 lemons, sliced
- 4 cloves garlic, minced
- 2 tbsp fresh thyme leaves
- 2 tbsp fresh rosemary leaves
- 2 tbsp olive oil
- Salt and black pepper, to taste

Preparation instructions:

1. Preheat the Air Fryer to 180°C for 5 minutes.
2. Rinse the whole chicken and pat it dry with paper towels.
3. In a bowl, mix together the minced garlic, fresh thyme, fresh rosemary, olive oil, salt, and black pepper.
4. Gently lift the skin of the chicken and rub the herb mixture under the skin and all over the chicken. Place the sliced lemons inside the chicken cavity.
5. Truss the chicken if desired.
6. Place the chicken in the air fryer basket breast side down.
7. Air fry at 180°C for about 30 minutes.
8. Flip the chicken and air fry for an additional 30 minutes or until the chicken's internal temperature reaches 75°C and the skin is crispy.
9. Let the chicken rest for a few minutes before carving.

Turkey and Cheese Empanadas

Serves: 4

Prep time: 25 minutes / Cook time: 15 minutes

Ingredients:

- 200g minced turkey
- 1 small onion, finely chopped
- 1 red pepper, finely chopped
- 100g shredded cheddar cheese
- 1 tsp ground cumin
- 1/2 tsp chilli powder
- Salt and black pepper, to taste
- 1 sheet puff pastry, thawed
- 1 egg, beaten

Preparation instructions:

1. Preheat the Air Fryer to 180°C for 5 minutes.
2. In a skillet, cook the minced turkey, chopped onion, and chopped red pepper until the turkey is cooked through and the vegetables are tender.
3. Stir in the shredded cheddar cheese, ground cumin, chilli powder, salt, and black pepper. Remove from heat.
4. Roll out the puff pastry and cut it into circles.
5. Place a spoonful of the turkey mixture on one side of each pastry circle.
6. Fold the other half of the pastry over the filling, forming a half-moon shape.
7. Seal the edges of the empanadas by pressing them with a fork. Brush the empanadas with the beaten egg. Place the empanadas in the air fryer basket.
8. Air fry at 180°C for about 15 minutes, until the empanadas are golden and crispy.
9. Serve the turkey and cheese empanadas.

Creamy Pesto Tortellini

Serves: 4

Prep time: 10 minutes / Cook time: 10 minutes

Ingredients:

- 300g cheese tortellini
- 60ml heavy cream
- 50g pesto sauce
- 50g grated Parmesan cheese
- Salt and black pepper, to taste
- Chopped fresh basil, for garnish

Preparation instructions:

1. Cook the cheese tortellini according to the package instructions. Drain and set aside.
2. Preheat the Air Fryer to 180°C for 5 minutes.
3. In a bowl, mix together the heavy cream, pesto

sauce, grated Parmesan cheese, salt, and black pepper.

4. Place the cooked tortellini in the air fryer basket.
5. Pour the creamy pesto mixture over the tortellini.
6. Air fry at 180°C for about 10 minutes, stirring occasionally, until the sauce is heated through and coats the tortellini.
7. Garnish with chopped fresh basil before serving.

Sweet and Sour Meatball Skewers

Serves: 4
Prep time: 20 minutes / Cook time: 15 minutes

Ingredients:

* 400g minced pork
* 120g breadcrumbs
* 1 egg
* 1/2 tsp garlic powder
* Salt and black pepper, to taste
* 1 red pepper, cut into chunks
* 1 green pepper, cut into chunks
* 1 small onion, cut into chunks
* 60ml sweet and sour sauce

Preparation instructions:

1. In a bowl, mix together the minced pork, breadcrumbs, egg, garlic powder, salt, and black pepper.
2. Shape the mixture into meatballs.
3. Preheat the Air Fryer to 180°C for 5 minutes.
4. Thread the meatballs, red pepper chunks, green pepper chunks, and onion chunks onto skewers.
5. Place the skewers in the air fryer basket.
6. Air fry at 180°C for about 15 minutes, turning the skewers halfway through, until the meatballs are cooked through and the vegetables are tender.
7. Brush the sweet and sour sauce over the skewers.
8. Air fry for an additional 2 minutes to caramelise the sauce.
9. Serve the sweet and sour meatball skewers.

Hawaiian BBQ Pork Chops

Serves: 4
Prep time: 15 minutes / Cook time: 20 minutes

Ingredients:

* 4 bone-in pork chops
* 120ml barbecue sauce
* 60ml pineapple juice
* 2 tbsp soy sauce
* 1 tbsp brown sugar
* 1 tsp minced ginger
* Salt and black pepper, to taste
* Sliced pineapple, for garnish

Preparation instructions:

1. Preheat the Air Fryer to 180°C for 5 minutes.
2. In a bowl, whisk together the barbecue sauce, pineapple juice, soy sauce, brown sugar, minced ginger, salt, and black pepper to make the marinade.
3. Place the pork chops in the marinade and let them marinate for about 10 minutes.
4. Place the marinated pork chops in the air fryer basket.
5. Air fry at 180°C for about 20 minutes, flipping the chops halfway through, until they're cooked through and have a nice caramelised glaze.
6. Garnish with sliced pineapple before serving.

Veggie-Packed Chicken Fried Rice

Serves: 4
Prep time: 15 minutes / Cook time: 15 minutes

Ingredients:

* 300g cooked and chilled rice
* 200g cooked chicken breast, diced
* 100g mixed vegetables (peas, carrots, corn)
* 2 eggs, beaten
* 60ml soy sauce
* 2 tsp sesame oil
* 1/2 tsp garlic powder
* 1/2 tsp onion powder
* Cooking oil

- Chopped green onions, for garnish

Preparation instructions:

1. Preheat the Air Fryer to 200°C for 5 minutes.
2. Heat a little cooking oil in a skillet or wok.
3. Add the mixed vegetables and cook until they're tender.
4. Push the vegetables to one side of the skillet and pour the beaten eggs into the empty side.
5. Scramble the eggs until they're cooked. Add the diced cooked chicken to the skillet and stir-fry briefly.
6. Add the chilled rice to the skillet and break up any clumps. Mix in the soy sauce, sesame oil, garlic powder, and onion powder. Stir-fry the fried rice until it's heated through and well combined.
7. Preheat the Air Fryer to 180°C for 5 minutes. Place the fried rice mixture in the air fryer basket.
8. Air fry at 180°C for about 5 minutes, stirring occasionally, until the fried rice is crispy and heated.
9. Garnish with chopped green onions before serving.

Spinach and Feta Stuffed Chicken Breast

Serves: 4
Prep time: 20 minutes / Cook time: 25 minutes

Ingredients:

- 4 boneless, skinless chicken breasts
- 100g spinach, cooked and squeezed dry
- 80g crumbled feta cheese
- 2 cloves garlic, minced
- 1 tsp dried oregano
- Salt and black pepper, to taste
- Cooking twine or toothpicks

Preparation instructions:

1. Preheat the Air Fryer to 180°C for 5 minutes.
2. In a bowl, mix together the cooked spinach, crumbled feta cheese, minced garlic, dried oregano, salt, and black pepper.

3. Gently butterfly each chicken breast by making a horizontal cut along one side and opening it like a book.
4. Stuff each chicken breast with the spinach and feta mixture.
5. Secure the stuffed chicken breasts with cooking twine or toothpicks.
6. Preheat the Air Fryer to 180°C for 5 minutes.
7. Lightly grease the air fryer basket with cooking oil.
8. Place the stuffed chicken breasts in the basket.
9. Air fry at 180°C for about 25 minutes, or until the chicken is cooked through and the internal temperature reaches 75°C. Remove the twine or toothpicks before serving.

Puffed Egg Tarts

Prep time: 10 minutes / Cook time: 42 minutes
Makes 4 tarts

Ingredients:

- Oil, for spraying
- Plain flour, for dusting
- 1 (340 g) sheet frozen puff pastry, thawed
- 180 ml shredded Cheddar cheese, divided
- 4 large eggs
- 2 teaspoons chopped fresh parsley
- Salt and freshly ground black pepper, to taste

Preparation instructions:

1. Preheat the air fryer to 200ºC.
2. Line the air fryer basket with parchment and spray lightly with oil.
3. Lightly dust your work surface with flour. Unfold the puff pastry and cut it into 4 equal squares.
4. Place 2 squares in the prepared basket. Cook for 10 minutes. Remove the basket.
5. Press the centre of each tart shell with a spoon to make an indentation. Sprinkle 3 tablespoons of cheese into each indentation and crack 1 egg into the centre of each tart shell. Cook for another 7 to 11 minutes, or until the eggs are cooked to your desired doneness.
6. Repeat with the remaining puff pastry squares,

cheese, and eggs. Sprinkle evenly with the parsley, and season with salt and black pepper.

7. Serve immediately.

Cajun Shrimp

Serves 4
Prep time: 15 minutes / Cook time: 9 minutes

Ingredients:

- Oil, for spraying
- 450 g jumbo raw shrimp, peeled and deveined
- 1 tablespoon Cajun seasoning
- 170 g cooked kielbasa, cut into thick slices
- ½ medium courgette, cut into ¼-inch-thick slices
- ½ medium yellow squash or butternut squash, cut into ¼-inch-thick slices
- 1 green pepper, seeded and cut into 1-inch pieces
- 2 tablespoons olive oil
- ½ teaspoon salt

Preparation instructions:

1. Preheat the air fryer to 204ºC.
2. Line the air fryer basket with parchment and spray lightly with oil.
3. In a large bowl, toss together the shrimp and Cajun seasoning. Add the kielbasa, courgette, squash, pepper, olive oil, and salt and mix well.
4. Transfer the mixture to the prepared basket, taking care not to overcrowd. You may need to work in batches, depending on the size of your air fryer.
5. Cook for 9 minutes, shaking and stirring every 3 minutes.
6. Serve immediately.

Coconut Chicken Tenders

Prep time: 10 minutes / Cook time: 12 minutes / Serves 4

Ingredients:

- Oil, for spraying
- 2 large eggs
- 60 ml milk
- 1 tablespoon hot sauce
- 350 ml sweetened flaked or desiccated coconut
- 180 ml panko breadcrumbs
- 1 teaspoon salt
- ½ teaspoon freshly ground black pepper
- 450 g chicken tenders

Preparation instructions:

1. Line the air fryer basket with parchment and spray lightly with oil.
2. In a small bowl, whisk together the eggs, milk, and hot sauce.
3. In a shallow dish, mix together the coconut, breadcrumbs, salt, and black pepper.
4. Coat the chicken in the egg mix, then dredge in the coconut mixture until evenly coated.
5. Place the chicken in the prepared basket and spray liberally with oil.
6. Air fry at 204ºC for 6 minutes, flip, spray with more oil, and cook for another 6 minutes, or until the internal temperature reaches 74ºC.

Cheesy Roasted Sweet Potatoes

Serves 4
Prep time: 7 minutes / Cook time: 18 to 23 minutes

Ingredients:

- 2 large sweet potatoes, peeled and sliced
- 1 teaspoon olive oil
- 1 tablespoon white balsamic vinegar
- 1 teaspoon dried thyme
- 60 ml grated Parmesan cheese

Preparation instructions:

1. In a large bowl, drizzle the sweet potato slices with the olive oil and toss.
2. Sprinkle with the balsamic vinegar and thyme and toss again.
3. Sprinkle the potatoes with the Parmesan cheese and toss to coat.
4. Roast the slices, in batches, in the air fryer basket at 204ºC for 18 to 23 minutes, tossing the sweet potato slices in the basket once during cooking, until tender.
5. Repeat with the remaining sweet potato slices.
6. Serve immediately.

Chapter 5: Fish and Seafood

Cajun Blackened Catfish

Serves: 4
Prep time: 10 minutes / Cook time: 10 minutes

Ingredients:
* 4 catfish fillets
* 2 tbsp Cajun seasoning
* 2 tbsp olive oil

Preparation instructions:
1. Preheat the Air Fryer to 200°C for 5 minutes.
2. Coat the catfish fillets with Cajun seasoning on both sides.
3. Drizzle olive oil over the fillets to help the seasoning stick.
4. Place the catfish fillets in the air fryer basket.
5. Air fry at 200°C for about 10 minutes or until the fish is cooked through and flakes easily.
6. Serve the Cajun blackened catfish with your choice of sides.

Lemon Garlic Butter Shrimp

Serves: 4
Prep time: 10 minutes / Cook time: 8 minutes

Ingredients:
* 400g large shrimp, peeled and deveined
* 2 tbsp melted butter
* 2 cloves garlic, minced
* Zest of 1 lemon
* Juice of 1 lemon
* Salt and black pepper, to taste
* Chopped fresh parsley, for garnish

Preparation instructions:
1. Preheat the Air Fryer to 180°C for 5 minutes.
2. In a bowl, mix together the melted butter, minced garlic, lemon zest, lemon juice, salt, and black pepper.
3. Toss the shrimp in the buttery mixture to coat.
4. Place the shrimp in the air fryer basket in a single layer.
5. Air fry at 180°C for about 8 minutes, flipping the shrimp halfway through, until they're pink and opaque.
6. Garnish with chopped fresh parsley before serving.

Crispy Breaded Fish Fillets

Serves: 4
Prep time: 15 minutes / Cook time: 15 minutes

Ingredients:
* 4 fish fillets (such as cod, haddock, or pollock)
* 60g breadcrumbs
* 30g grated Parmesan cheese
* 1 tsp dried parsley
* 1/2 tsp garlic powder
* Salt and black pepper, to taste
* 1 egg, beaten

Preparation instructions:
1. Preheat the Air Fryer to 200°C for 5 minutes.
2. In a bowl, mix together the breadcrumbs, grated Parmesan cheese, dried parsley, garlic powder, salt, and black pepper.
3. Dip each fish fillet into the beaten egg, then coat with the breadcrumb mixture.
4. Place the coated fish fillets in the air fryer basket.
5. Air fry at 200°C for about 15 minutes or until the fish is golden and crispy, and the internal temperature reaches 63°C.
6. Serve the crispy breaded fish fillets with your favourite tartar sauce.

Coconut-Crusted Cod

Serves: 4
Prep time: 15 minutes / Cook time: 15 minutes

Ingredients:
* 4 cod fillets
* 60g shredded coconut
* 30g breadcrumbs
* 1 tsp curry powder
* Salt and black pepper, to taste
* 1 egg, beaten

Preparation instructions:
1. Preheat the Air Fryer to 200°C for 5 minutes.
2. In a bowl, mix together the shredded coconut, breadcrumbs, curry powder, salt, and black pepper.
3. Dip each cod fillet into the beaten egg, then coat with the coconut-breadcrumb mixture.

4. Place the coated cod fillets in the air fryer basket.
5. Air fry at 200°C for about 15 minutes or until the fish is cooked through and flakes easily.
6. Serve the coconut-crusted cod with a squeeze of lime.

Sesame Ginger Glazed Salmon

Serves: 4

Prep time: 10 minutes / Cook time: 12 minutes

Ingredients:
- 4 salmon fillets
- 60ml soy sauce
- 2 tbsp honey
- 1 tbsp sesame oil
- 1 tsp minced ginger
- 1 clove garlic, minced
- 1 tsp sesame seeds
- Chopped green onions, for garnish

Preparation instructions:
1. Preheat the Air Fryer to 180°C for 5 minutes.
2. In a bowl, whisk together the soy sauce, honey, sesame oil, minced ginger, and minced garlic to make the glaze.
3. Place the salmon fillets in the air fryer basket.
4. Brush the glaze over the salmon fillets.
5. Air fry at 180°C for about 12 minutes or until the salmon is cooked through and flakes easily.
6. Sprinkle sesame seeds and chopped green onions over the glazed salmon before serving.

Spicy Buffalo Shrimp

Serves: 4

Prep time: 10 minutes / Cook time: 8 minutes

Ingredients:
- 400g large shrimp, peeled and deveined
- 60ml hot sauce (such as buffalo sauce)
- 2 tbsp melted butter
- 1 tsp Worcestershire sauce
- 1/2 tsp garlic powder
- Salt and black pepper, to taste

Preparation instructions:
1. Preheat the Air Fryer to 180°C for 5 minutes.
2. In a bowl, mix together the hot sauce, melted butter, Worcestershire sauce, garlic powder, salt, and black pepper.

3. Toss the shrimp in the spicy sauce to coat.
4. Place the shrimp in the air fryer basket in a single layer.
5. Air fry at 180°C for about 8 minutes, flipping the shrimp halfway through, until they're pink and opaque.
6. Serve the spicy buffalo shrimp with celery sticks and blue cheese dressing.

Herb-Marinated Grilled Swordfish

Serves: 4

Prep time: 15 minutes / Cook time: 10 minutes

Ingredients:
- 4 swordfish steaks
- 2 tbsp olive oil
- 2 tbsp lemon juice
- 2 cloves garlic, minced
- 1 tsp dried thyme
- 1 tsp dried oregano
- Salt and black pepper, to taste
- Lemon wedges, for serving

Preparation instructions:
1. In a bowl, mix together the olive oil, lemon juice, minced garlic, dried thyme, dried oregano, salt, and black pepper to make the marinade.
2. Coat the swordfish steaks with the marinade and let them marinate for about 10 minutes.
3. Preheat the Air Fryer to 200°C for 5 minutes.
4. Place the swordfish steaks in the air fryer basket.
5. Air fry at 200°C for about 10 minutes or until the fish is cooked through and flakes easily.
6. Serve the herb-marinated grilled swordfish with lemon wedges.

Teriyaki Glazed Mahi-Mahi

Serves: 4

Prep time: 10 minutes / Cook time: 12 minutes

Ingredients:
- 4 mahi-mahi fillets
- 60ml teriyaki sauce
- 2 tbsp honey
- 1 tbsp soy sauce
- 1 tsp minced ginger
- 1 clove garlic, minced
- 1/2 tsp sesame oil

- Chopped green onions, for garnish

Preparation instructions:
1. Preheat the Air Fryer to 180°C for 5 minutes.
2. In a bowl, mix together the teriyaki sauce, honey, soy sauce, minced ginger, minced garlic, and sesame oil to make the glaze.
3. Place the mahi-mahi fillets in the air fryer basket.
4. Brush the glaze over the mahi-mahi fillets.
5. Air fry at 180°C for about 12 minutes or until the fish is cooked through and flakes easily.
6. Garnish with chopped green onions before serving.

Zesty Lemon Pepper Tilapia

Serves: 4
Prep time: 10 minutes / Cook time: 10 minutes

Ingredients:
- 4 tilapia fillets
- Zest of 1 lemon
- Juice of 1 lemon
- 2 tbsp olive oil
- 1 tsp lemon pepper seasoning
- Salt, to taste
- Fresh lemon slices, for garnish

Preparation instructions:
1. Preheat the Air Fryer to 200°C for 5 minutes.
2. In a bowl, mix together the lemon zest, lemon juice, olive oil, lemon pepper seasoning, and salt.
3. Coat the tilapia fillets with the lemon mixture.
4. Place the tilapia fillets in the air fryer basket.
5. Air fry at 200°C for about 10 minutes or until the fish is cooked through and flakes easily.
6. Garnish with fresh lemon slices before serving.

Garlic Parmesan Air-Fried Scallops

Serves: 4
Prep time: 10 minutes / Cook time: 6 minutes

Ingredients:
- 300g fresh scallops
- 2 tbsp melted butter
- 2 cloves garlic, minced
- 30g grated Parmesan cheese
- 2 tbsp chopped fresh parsley

- Salt and black pepper, to taste
- Lemon wedges, for serving

Preparation instructions:
1. Preheat the Air Fryer to 200°C for 5 minutes.
2. In a bowl, mix together the melted butter, minced garlic, grated Parmesan cheese, chopped parsley, salt, and black pepper.
3. Pat the scallops dry with paper towels.
4. Toss the scallops in the buttery mixture to coat.
5. Place the scallops in the air fryer basket in a single layer.
6. Air fry at 200°C for about 6 minutes, shaking the basket halfway through, until the scallops are opaque and slightly golden.
7. Serve the garlic Parmesan air-fried scallops with lemon wedges.

Tandoori-Style Grilled Prawns

Serves: 4
Prep time: 15 minutes / Cook time: 8 minutes

Ingredients:
- 300g large prawns, peeled and deveined
- 60ml plain yoghurt
- 1 tbsp tandoori spice mix
- 1 tsp minced ginger
- 1 tsp minced garlic
- 1/2 tsp ground cumin
- 1/4 tsp ground coriander
- Salt and black pepper, to taste
- Lemon wedges, for serving

Preparation instructions:
1. In a bowl, mix together the plain yoghurt, tandoori spice mix, minced ginger, minced garlic, ground cumin, ground coriander, salt, and black pepper to make the marinade.
2. Add the prawns to the marinade and coat them well.
3. Preheat the Air Fryer to 200°C for 5 minutes.
4. Thread the marinated prawns on skewers.
5. Place the prawn skewers in the air fryer basket.
6. Air fry at 200°C for about 8 minutes, turning the skewers halfway through, until the prawns are cooked and charred.
7. Serve the tandoori-style grilled prawns with lemon wedges.

Mediterranean Grilled Sardines

Serves: 4

Prep time: 10 minutes / Cook time: 10 minutes

Ingredients:

- 8 fresh sardines, gutted and cleaned
- 2 tbsp olive oil
- 2 cloves garlic, minced
- 1 tsp dried oregano
- 1/2 tsp dried thyme
- 1/2 tsp paprika
- Salt and black pepper, to taste
- Lemon wedges, for serving

Preparation instructions:

1. Preheat the Air Fryer to 200°C for 5 minutes.
2. In a bowl, mix together the olive oil, minced garlic, dried oregano, dried thyme, paprika, salt, and black pepper to make the marinade.
3. Pat the sardines dry with paper towels.
4. Coat the sardines with the marinade.
5. Place the sardines in the air fryer basket in a single layer.
6. Air fry at 200°C for about 10 minutes, turning the sardines halfway through, until they're cooked and crispy.
7. Serve the Mediterranean grilled sardines with lemon wedges.

Honey Mustard Glazed Trout

Serves: 4

Prep time: 10 minutes / Cook time: 12 minutes

Ingredients:

- 4 trout fillets
- 2 tbsp honey
- 2 tbsp Dijon mustard
- 1 tbsp olive oil
- 1 clove garlic, minced
- 1 tsp minced fresh thyme
- Salt and black pepper, to taste
- Lemon wedges, for serving

Preparation instructions:

1. Preheat the Air Fryer to 200°C for 5 minutes.
2. In a bowl, whisk together the honey, Dijon mustard, olive oil, minced garlic, minced fresh thyme, salt, and black pepper to make the glaze.
3. Coat the trout fillets with the glaze.
4. Place the trout fillets in the air fryer basket.
5. Air fry at 200°C for about 12 minutes or until the trout is cooked through and flakes easily.
6. Serve the honey mustard glazed trout with lemon wedges.

Pistachio-Crusted Halibut

Serves: 4

Prep time: 15 minutes / Cook time: 12 minutes

Ingredients:

- 4 halibut fillets
- 60g shelled pistachios, finely chopped
- 30g breadcrumbs
- 1 tsp dried parsley
- 1/2 tsp garlic powder
- Salt and black pepper, to taste
- 1 egg, beaten

Preparation instructions:

1. Preheat the Air Fryer to 200°C for 5 minutes.
2. In a bowl, mix together the chopped pistachios, breadcrumbs, dried parsley, garlic powder, salt, and black pepper.
3. Dip each halibut fillet into the beaten egg, then coat with the pistachio-breadcrumb mixture.
4. Place the coated halibut fillets in the air fryer basket.
5. Air fry at 200°C for about 12 minutes or until the fish is cooked through and flakes easily.
6. Serve the pistachio-crusted halibut with a sprinkle of extra chopped pistachios.

Thai Red Curry Sea Bass

Serves: 4

Prep time: 15 minutes / Cook time: 12 minutes

Ingredients:

- 4 sea bass fillets
- 60ml coconut milk
- 1 tbsp Thai red curry paste
- 1 tsp fish sauce
- 1 tsp brown sugar
- 1 tsp minced ginger
- 1 tsp minced lemongrass
- Fresh coriander leaves, for garnish

Preparation instructions:

1. In a bowl, mix together the coconut milk, Thai red curry paste, fish sauce, brown sugar, minced ginger, and minced lemongrass to make the marinade.
2. Coat the sea bass fillets with the marinade and let them marinate for about 10 minutes.
3. Preheat the Air Fryer to 200°C for 5 minutes.
4. Place the sea bass fillets in the air fryer basket.
5. Air fry at 200°C for about 12 minutes or until the fish is cooked through and flakes easily.
6. Garnish with fresh coriander leaves before serving.

Chimichurri Grilled Tuna Steaks

Serves: 4
Prep time: 15 minutes / Cook time: 10 minutes

Ingredients:

- 4 tuna steaks
- 60ml olive oil
- 2 tbsp red wine vinegar
- 120g chopped fresh parsley
- 2 cloves garlic, minced
- 1 tsp dried oregano
- 1/2 tsp crushed red pepper flakes
- Salt and black pepper, to taste

Preparation instructions:

1. In a bowl, whisk together the olive oil, red wine vinegar, chopped fresh parsley, minced garlic, dried oregano, crushed red pepper flakes, salt, and black pepper to make the chimichurri sauce.
2. Coat the tuna steaks with the chimichurri sauce and let them marinate for about 10 minutes.
3. Preheat the Air Fryer to 200°C for 5 minutes.
4. Place the tuna steaks in the air fryer basket.
5. Air fry at 200°C for about 10 minutes or until the tuna is cooked to your desired level of doneness.
6. Serve the chimichurri grilled tuna steaks with extra sauce on top.

Herbed Baked Salmon Patties

Serves: 4
Prep time: 15 minutes / Cook time: 10 minutes

Ingredients:

- 400g canned salmon, drained and flaked
- 60g breadcrumbs
- 1 egg
- 2 tbsp chopped fresh dill
- 2 tbsp chopped fresh parsley
- 1 tbsp lemon juice
- 1/2 tsp onion powder
- Salt and black pepper, to taste
- Cooking oil

Preparation instructions:

1. In a bowl, mix together the canned salmon, breadcrumbs, egg, chopped fresh dill, chopped fresh parsley, lemon juice, onion powder, salt, and black pepper.
2. Form the mixture into patties.
3. Preheat the Air Fryer to 200°C for 5 minutes.
4. Lightly grease the air fryer basket with cooking oil.
5. Place the salmon patties in the basket.
6. Air fry at 200°C for about 10 minutes, flipping the patties halfway through, until they're golden and heated through.
7. Serve the herbed baked salmon patties with a squeeze of lemon.

Almond-Crusted Dijon Fish

Serves: 4
Prep time: 15 minutes / Cook time: 12 minutes

Ingredients:

- 4 white fish fillets (such as cod or haddock)
- 60g ground almonds
- 30g breadcrumbs
- 2 tbsp Dijon mustard
- 1 tsp dried thyme
- 1/2 tsp garlic powder
- Salt and black pepper, to taste
- Lemon wedges, for serving

Preparation instructions:

1. Preheat the Air Fryer to 200°C for 5 minutes.
2. In a bowl, mix together the ground almonds, breadcrumbs, Dijon mustard, dried thyme, garlic powder, salt, and black pepper.
3. Coat each fish fillet with the almond mixture.
4. Place the coated fish fillets in the air fryer basket.
5. Air fry at 200°C for about 12 minutes or until the fish is cooked through and flakes easily.
6. Serve the almond-crusted Dijon fish with lemon wedges.

Coconut Curry Cod with Mango Salsa

Serves: 4

Prep time: 15 minutes / Cook time: 12 minutes

Ingredients:

For the Coconut Curry Cod:
- 600g cod fillets
- 200ml coconut milk
- 2 tbsp curry powder
- 1 tbsp lime juice
- 1 tbsp soy sauce
- 2 cloves garlic, minced
- 1 tsp grated ginger
- 1/2 tsp turmeric powder
- 1/2 tsp cumin powder
- 1/2 tsp paprika
- Salt and black pepper, to taste

For the Mango Salsa:
- 1 ripe mango, diced
- 1/2 red onion, finely chopped
- 1/2 red bell pepper, diced
- 1/2 green bell pepper, diced
- 2 tbsp chopped fresh cilantro
- 1 tbsp lime juice
- 1 tbsp olive oil
- Salt, to taste

Preparation instructions:

1. Preheat the Air Fryer to 200°C for 5 minutes.
2. In a bowl, combine the coconut milk, curry powder, lime juice, soy sauce, minced garlic, grated ginger, turmeric powder, cumin powder, paprika, salt, and black pepper. Stir well to make the coconut curry marinade.
3. Pat dry the cod fillets using paper towels. Place the cod fillets in a shallow dish and pour the coconut curry marinade over them, ensuring the fillets are coated evenly. Let them marinate for 10 minutes.
4. While the cod is marinating, prepare the mango salsa. In a separate bowl, combine the diced mango, finely chopped red onion, diced red bell pepper, diced green bell pepper, chopped fresh cilantro, lime juice, olive oil, and salt. Toss well to mix all the ingredients. Set aside.
5. Place the marinated cod fillets in the Air Fryer basket, ensuring they are not overcrowded. Air fry at 200°C for 10-12 minutes or until the cod is cooked through and flakes easily with a fork.
6. Once cooked, remove the cod from the Air Fryer and let it rest for a minute.
7. Serve the coconut curry cod with a generous scoop of mango salsa on top. Enjoy this delightful and flavorful coconut curry cod with vibrant mango salsa!

Teriyaki Glazed Mahi-Mahi with Pineapple Salsa

Serves: 4

Prep time: 15 minutes / Cook time: 10 minutes

Ingredients:

For the Teriyaki Glazed Mahi-Mahi:
- 600g mahi-mahi fillets
- 4 tbsp teriyaki sauce
- 2 tbsp honey
- 1 tbsp soy sauce
- 1 tbsp rice vinegar
- 1 tbsp grated ginger
- 2 cloves garlic, minced
- 1/4 tsp black pepper

For the Pineapple Salsa:
- 240g diced fresh pineapple
- 60g diced red bell pepper
- 60g diced yellow bell pepper
- 60g diced red onion
- 2 tbsp chopped fresh cilantro
- 1 tbsp lime juice
- 1/2 tsp honey
- 1/4 tsp salt

Preparation instructions:

1. Preheat the Air Fryer to 200°C for 5 minutes.
2. In a bowl, whisk together the teriyaki sauce, honey, soy sauce, rice vinegar, grated ginger, minced garlic, and black pepper to make the teriyaki glaze.
3. Pat dry the mahi-mahi fillets using paper towels.

Brush both sides of the fillets with the teriyaki glaze.

4. In another bowl, combine the diced fresh pineapple, diced red bell pepper, diced yellow bell pepper, diced red onion, chopped fresh cilantro, lime juice, honey, and salt to make the pineapple salsa. Mix well to combine all the ingredients.

5. Place the marinated mahi-mahi fillets in the Air Fryer basket, ensuring they are not overcrowded. Air fry at 200°C for 8-10 minutes or until the fish is cooked through and flakes easily with a fork.

6. Once cooked, remove the mahi-mahi from the Air Fryer and let it rest for a minute.

7. Serve the teriyaki glazed mahi-mahi with a generous scoop of pineapple salsa on top. Enjoy this delicious and tangy teriyaki glazed fish with the vibrant flavours of pineapple salsa!

8. Note: Adjust the cooking time depending on the thickness of the mahi-mahi fillets. Thicker fillets may require additional cooking time.

Almond-Crusted Fish

Serves 4
Prep time: 15 minutes / Cook time: 10 minutes

Ingredients:
- 4 firm white fish fillets, 110g each
- 45 g breadcrumbs
- 20 g slivered almonds, crushed
- 2 tablespoons lemon juice
- ⅛ teaspoon cayenne
- Salt and pepper, to taste
- 940 g plain flour
- 1 egg, beaten with 1 tablespoon water
- Olive or vegetable oil for misting or cooking spray

Preparation instructions:
1. Split fish fillets lengthwise down the center to create 8 pieces.
2. Mix breadcrumbs and almonds together and set aside.
3. Mix the lemon juice and cayenne together. Brush on all sides of fish.
4. Season fish to taste with salt and pepper.
5. Place the flour on a sheet of wax paper.
6. Roll fillets in flour, dip in egg wash, and roll in the crumb mixture.
7. Mist both sides of fish with oil or cooking spray.
8. Spray the air fryer basket and lay fillets inside.
9. Roast at 200ºC for 5 minutes, turn fish over, and cook for an additional 5 minutes or until fish is done and flakes easily.

chilli Lime Prawns

Serves 4
Prep time: 5 minutes / Cook time: 5 minutes

Ingredients:
- 455 g medium prawns, peeled and deveined
- 1 tablespoon salted butter, melted
- 2 teaspoons chilli powder
- ¼ teaspoon garlic powder
- ¼ teaspoon salt
- ¼ teaspoon ground black pepper
- ½ small lime, zested and juiced, divided

Preparation instructions:
1. In a medium bowl, toss prawns with butter, then sprinkle with chilli powder, garlic powder, salt, pepper, and lime zest.
2. Place prawns into ungreased air fryer basket. Adjust the temperature to 204ºC and air fry for 5 minutes. Prawns will be firm and form a "C" shape when done.
3. Transfer prawns to a large serving dish and drizzle with lime juice. Serve warm.

Chapter 6: Meat and Poultry Dishes

Tender Rosemary Roast Beef

Serves: 4
Prep time: 15 minutes / Cook time: 30 minutes

Ingredients:

- 500g beef roast (such as sirloin or ribeye)
- 2 tbsp olive oil
- 2 cloves garlic, minced
- 1 tbsp chopped fresh rosemary
- Salt and black pepper, to taste

Preparation instructions:

1. Preheat the Air Fryer to 200°C for 5 minutes.
2. In a bowl, mix together the olive oil, minced garlic, chopped fresh rosemary, salt, and black pepper.
3. Rub the rosemary mixture over the beef roast to coat it evenly.
4. Place the beef roast in the air fryer basket.
5. Air fry at 200°C for about 30 minutes or until the beef reaches your desired level of doneness.
6. Let the roast beef rest for a few minutes before slicing.

Spicy Korean-Style Chicken Wings

Serves: 4
Prep time: 15 minutes / Cook time: 25 minutes

Ingredients:

- 800g chicken wings
- 3 tbsp gochujang (Korean red pepper paste)
- 2 tbsp soy sauce
- 2 tbsp honey
- 1 tbsp sesame oil
- 2 cloves garlic, minced
- 1 tsp minced ginger
- Toasted sesame seeds, for garnish
- Sliced green onions, for garnish

Preparation instructions:

1. In a bowl, whisk together the gochujang, soy sauce, honey, sesame oil, minced garlic, and minced ginger to make the marinade.
2. Coat the chicken wings with the marinade and let them marinate for about 10 minutes.
3. Preheat the Air Fryer to 200°C for 5 minutes.
4. Place the marinated chicken wings in the air fryer basket.
5. Air fry at 200°C for about 25 minutes or until the chicken wings are cooked through and crispy.
6. Garnish with toasted sesame seeds and sliced green onions before serving.

Maple Glazed Bacon-Wrapped Chicken

Serves: 4
Prep time: 15 minutes / Cook time: 20 minutes

Ingredients:

- 4 boneless chicken breasts
- 8 slices bacon
- 3 tbsp maple syrup
- 2 tbsp Dijon mustard
- 1 tsp minced garlic
- Salt and black pepper, to taste

Preparation instructions:

1. Preheat the Air Fryer to 200°C for 5 minutes.
2. In a bowl, mix together the maple syrup, Dijon mustard, minced garlic, salt, and black pepper to make the glaze.
3. Wrap each chicken breast with 2 slices of bacon.
4. Brush the bacon-wrapped chicken with the maple glaze.
5. Place the bacon-wrapped chicken in the air fryer basket.
6. Air fry at 200°C for about 20 minutes or until the chicken is cooked through and the bacon is crispy.

Balsamic Glazed Pork Tenderloin

Serves: 4
Prep time: 15 minutes / Cook time: 25 minutes

Ingredients:
- 500g pork tenderloin
- 3 tbsp balsamic vinegar
- 2 tbsp olive oil
- 1 tbsp honey
- 1 tsp minced garlic
- 1/2 tsp dried thyme
- Salt and black pepper, to taste

Preparation instructions:
1. Preheat the Air Fryer to 200°C for 5 minutes.
2. In a bowl, whisk together the balsamic vinegar, olive oil, honey, minced garlic, dried thyme, salt, and black pepper to make the glaze.
3. Coat the pork tenderloin with the balsamic glaze.
4. Place the pork tenderloin in the air fryer basket.
5. Air fry at 200°C for about 25 minutes or until the pork is cooked through and reaches an internal temperature of 63°C.
6. Let the pork tenderloin rest for a few minutes before slicing.

Tangy Orange Glazed Ribs

Serves: 4
Prep time: 15 minutes / Cook time: 30 minutes

Ingredients:
- 800g pork ribs
- 120 ml orange marmalade
- 2 tbsp soy sauce
- 2 tbsp rice vinegar
- 1 tbsp minced ginger
- 1 tsp minced garlic
- Chopped fresh coriander, for garnish

Preparation instructions:
1. Preheat the Air Fryer to 200°C for 5 minutes.
2. In a bowl, mix together the orange marmalade, soy sauce, rice vinegar, minced ginger, and minced garlic to make the glaze.
3. Brush the glaze over the pork ribs.
4. Place the pork ribs in the air fryer basket.
5. Air fry at 200°C for about 30 minutes or until the ribs are cooked through and glazed.
6. Garnish with chopped fresh coriander before serving.

Garlic and Herb Butter Turkey Breast

Serves: 4
Prep time: 15 minutes / Cook time: 35 minutes

Ingredients:
- 500g turkey breast
- 3 tbsp melted butter
- 2 cloves garlic, minced
- 1 tbsp chopped fresh sage
- 1 tbsp chopped fresh thyme
- Salt and black pepper, to taste

Preparation instructions:
1. Preheat the Air Fryer to 180°C for 5 minutes.
2. In a bowl, mix together the melted butter, minced garlic, chopped fresh sage, chopped fresh thyme, salt, and black pepper.
3. Rub the garlic and herb butter mixture over the turkey breast to coat it evenly.
4. Place the turkey breast in the air fryer basket.
5. Air fry at 180°C for about 35 minutes or until the turkey is cooked through and reaches an internal temperature of 75°C.
6. Let the turkey breast rest for a few minutes before slicing.

Moroccan Spiced Lamb Chops

Serves: 4
Prep time: 15 minutes / Cook time: 12 minutes

Ingredients:
- 8 lamb chops
- 2 tbsp olive oil
- 1 tsp ground cumin
- 1 tsp ground coriander
- 1/2 tsp ground cinnamon
- 1/2 tsp paprika
- 1/4 tsp ground ginger
- Salt and black pepper, to taste
- Chopped fresh mint, for garnish

Preparation instructions:
1. Preheat the Air Fryer to 200°C for 5 minutes.

2. In a bowl, mix together the olive oil, ground cumin, ground coriander, ground cinnamon, paprika, ground ginger, salt, and black pepper to make the spice mixture.
3. Coat the lamb chops with the spice mixture.
4. Place the lamb chops in the air fryer basket.
5. Air fry at 200°C for about 12 minutes or until the lamb chops are cooked to your desired level of doneness.
6. Garnish with chopped fresh mint before serving.

Chipotle Lime Grilled Steak

Serves: 4

Prep time: 15 minutes / Cook time: 15 minutes

Ingredients:
- 4 beef steak cuts (such as ribeye or sirloin)
- 2 tbsp olive oil
- Juice of 1 lime
- 2 tsp chipotle chilli powder
- 1 tsp minced garlic
- 1/2 tsp ground cumin
- Salt and black pepper, to taste

Preparation instructions:
1. Preheat the Air Fryer to 200°C for 5 minutes.
2. In a bowl, whisk together the olive oil, lime juice, chipotle chilli powder, minced garlic, ground cumin, salt, and black pepper to make the marinade.
3. Coat the beef steak cuts with the marinade.
4. Place the steak cuts in the air fryer basket.
5. Air fry at 200°C for about 15 minutes or until the steaks are cooked to your desired level of doneness.
6. Let the steaks rest for a few minutes before slicing.

Honey Sriracha Glazed Chicken Thighs

Serves: 4

Prep time: 15 minutes / Cook time: 20 minutes

Ingredients:
- 8 bone-in chicken thighs
- 3 tbsp honey
- 2 tbsp Sriracha sauce
- 1 tbsp soy sauce
- 1 tsp minced garlic
- 1/2 tsp minced ginger
- Chopped fresh coriander, for garnish

Preparation instructions:
1. Preheat the Air Fryer to 200°C for 5 minutes.
2. In a bowl, whisk together the honey, Sriracha sauce, soy sauce, minced garlic, and minced ginger to make the glaze.
3. Coat the chicken thighs with the glaze.
4. Place the chicken thighs in the air fryer basket.
5. Air fry at 200°C for about 20 minutes or until the chicken thighs are cooked through and the glaze is caramelised.
6. Garnish with chopped fresh coriander before serving.

Mediterranean Herb Lamb Kebabs

Serves: 4

Prep time: 15 minutes / Cook time: 15 minutes

Ingredients:
- 500g lamb cubes (shoulder or leg)
- 2 tbsp olive oil
- 1 tsp dried oregano
- 1 tsp dried thyme
- 1/2 tsp dried rosemary
- 1/2 tsp paprika
- Salt and black pepper, to taste
- Lemon wedges, for serving

Preparation instructions:
1. Preheat the Air Fryer to 200°C for 5 minutes.
2. In a bowl, mix together the olive oil, dried oregano, dried thyme, dried rosemary, paprika, salt, and black pepper to make the herb mixture.
3. Coat the lamb cubes with the herb mixture.
4. Thread the lamb cubes onto skewers.
5. Place the lamb kebabs in the air fryer basket.
6. Air fry at 200°C for about 15 minutes or until the lamb is cooked to your desired level of

doneness.

7. Serve the Mediterranean herb lamb kebabs with lemon wedges.

Jamaican Jerk Chicken Drumsticks

Serves: 4

Prep time: 15 minutes / Cook time: 25 minutes

Ingredients:

- 8 chicken drumsticks
- 2 tbsp Jamaican jerk seasoning
- 2 tbsp olive oil
- 1 tbsp soy sauce
- 1 tbsp lime juice
- 1 tsp brown sugar
- Salt and black pepper, to taste

Preparation instructions:

1. Preheat the Air Fryer to 200°C for 5 minutes.
2. In a bowl, mix together the Jamaican jerk seasoning, olive oil, soy sauce, lime juice, brown sugar, salt, and black pepper to make the marinade.
3. Coat the chicken drumsticks with the marinade.
4. Place the drumsticks in the air fryer basket.
5. Air fry at 200°C for about 25 minutes or until the chicken is cooked through and the skin is crispy.

Smoky BBQ Pork Belly Slices

Serves: 4

Prep time: 15 minutes / Cook time: 25 minutes

Ingredients:

- 500g pork belly slices
- 3 tbsp smoky BBQ sauce
- 1 tbsp olive oil
- 1 tsp smoked paprika
- 1/2 tsp garlic powder
- Salt and black pepper, to taste

Preparation instructions:

1. Preheat the Air Fryer to 200°C for 5 minutes.
2. In a bowl, mix together the smoky BBQ sauce, olive oil, smoked paprika, garlic powder, salt, and black pepper.
3. Coat the pork belly slices with the BBQ sauce mixture.
4. Place the pork slices in the air fryer basket.
5. Air fry at 200°C for about 25 minutes or until the pork is cooked through and the edges are crispy.

Teriyaki Pineapple Turkey Burgers

Serves: 4

Prep time: 15 minutes / Cook time: 15 minutes

Ingredients:

- 500g minced turkey
- 120g finely chopped pineapple
- 3 tbsp teriyaki sauce
- 2 tbsp breadcrumbs
- 1 tsp minced garlic
- 1/2 tsp minced ginger
- Salt and black pepper, to taste
- Burger buns and toppings, for serving

Preparation instructions:

1. Preheat the Air Fryer to 200°C for 5 minutes.
2. In a bowl, mix together the minced turkey, chopped pineapple, teriyaki sauce, breadcrumbs, minced garlic, minced ginger, salt, and black pepper.
3. Form the mixture into burger patties.
4. Place the turkey burger patties in the air fryer basket.
5. Air fry at 200°C for about 15 minutes or until the burgers are cooked through.
6. Serve the teriyaki pineapple turkey burgers on buns with your favourite toppings.

Italian Herb Marinated Pork Chops

Serves: 4

Prep time: 15 minutes / Cook time: 20 minutes

Ingredients:

- 4 pork chops

- 3 tbsp olive oil
- 2 tbsp balsamic vinegar
- 1 tsp dried oregano
- 1 tsp dried basil
- 1/2 tsp dried rosemary
- 1/2 tsp dried thyme
- Salt and black pepper, to taste

Preparation instructions:

1. Preheat the Air Fryer to 200°C for 5 minutes.
2. In a bowl, whisk together the olive oil, balsamic vinegar, dried oregano, dried basil, dried rosemary, dried thyme, salt, and black pepper to make the marinade.
3. Coat the pork chops with the marinade.
4. Place the pork chops in the air fryer basket.
5. Air fry at 200°C for about 20 minutes or until the pork chops are cooked through and juicy.

Cajun Spiced Chicken Quarters

Serves: 4
Prep time: 15 minutes / Cook time: 30 minutes

Ingredients:

- 4 chicken leg quarters
- 2 tbsp Cajun seasoning
- 1 tbsp olive oil
- 1 tsp smoked paprika
- 1/2 tsp garlic powder
- 1/2 tsp onion powder
- Salt and black pepper, to taste

Preparation instructions:

1. Preheat the Air Fryer to 200°C for 5 minutes.
2. In a bowl, mix together the Cajun seasoning, olive oil, smoked paprika, garlic powder, onion powder, salt, and black pepper.
3. Coat the chicken leg quarters with the spice mixture.
4. Place the chicken quarters in the air fryer basket.
5. Air fry at 200°C for about 30 minutes or until the chicken is cooked through and the skin is crispy.

Blackberry Balsamic Glazed Duck Breast

Serves: 4
Prep time: 15 minutes / Cook time: 20 minutes

Ingredients:

- 4 duck breast fillets
- 120g blackberries
- 3 tbsp balsamic vinegar
- 2 tbsp honey
- 1 tsp minced garlic
- Salt and black pepper, to taste

Preparation instructions:

1. Preheat the Air Fryer to 200°C for 5 minutes.
2. In a small saucepan, combine the blackberries, balsamic vinegar, honey, minced garlic, salt, and black pepper. Cook over medium heat until the blackberries break down and the mixture thickens to a glaze.
3. Coat the duck breast fillets with the blackberry balsamic glaze.
4. Place the duck fillets in the air fryer basket.
5. Air fry at 200°C for about 20 minutes or until the duck is cooked to your desired level of doneness.

Rosemary and Garlic Stuffed Pork Loin

Serves: 4
Prep time: 15 minutes / Cook time: 30 minutes

Ingredients:

- 500g pork loin
- 4 cloves garlic, minced
- 2 tbsp chopped fresh rosemary
- 2 tbsp olive oil
- Salt and black pepper, to taste

Preparation instructions:

1. Preheat the Air Fryer to 200°C for 5 minutes.
2. In a bowl, mix together the minced garlic, chopped fresh rosemary, olive oil, salt, and black pepper to make the stuffing.

3. Cut a slit along the length of the pork loin to create a pocket for the stuffing.
4. Stuff the garlic and rosemary mixture into the pocket.
5. Place the stuffed pork loin in the air fryer basket.
6. Air fry at 200°C for about 30 minutes or until the pork loin is cooked through and tender.

Greek-Inspired Lemon Chicken Skewers

Serves: 4

Prep time: 15 minutes / Cook time: 15 minutes

Ingredients:

- 500g boneless chicken breast, cut into cubes
- 2 tbsp olive oil
- Juice of 1 lemon
- 1 tsp dried oregano
- 1 tsp minced garlic
- Salt and black pepper, to taste
- Tzatziki sauce, for serving

Preparation instructions:

1. Preheat the Air Fryer to 200°C for 5 minutes.
2. In a bowl, whisk together the olive oil, lemon juice, dried oregano, minced garlic, salt, and black pepper to make the marinade.
3. Coat the chicken cubes with the marinade.
4. Thread the chicken cubes onto skewers.
5. Place the chicken skewers in the air fryer basket.
6. Air fry at 200°C for about 15 minutes or until the chicken is cooked through.
7. Serve the Greek-inspired lemon chicken skewers with tzatziki sauce.

Honey Dijon Glazed Ham Steaks

Serves: 4

Prep time: 15 minutes / Cook time: 20 minutes

Ingredients:

- 4 ham steaks
- 3 tbsp honey
- 2 tbsp Dijon mustard

- 1 tbsp apple cider vinegar
- 1/2 tsp minced garlic
- Salt and black pepper, to taste

Preparation instructions:

1. Preheat the Air Fryer to 200°C for 5 minutes.
2. In a bowl, whisk together the honey, Dijon mustard, apple cider vinegar, minced garlic, salt, and black pepper to make the glaze.
3. Coat the ham steaks with the honey Dijon glaze.
4. Place the ham steaks in the air fryer basket.
5. Air fry at 200°C for about 20 minutes or until the ham is heated through and glazed.

Five-Spice Crispy Duck Legs

Serves: 4

Prep time: 15 minutes / Cook time: 40 minutes

Ingredients:

- 4 duck leg quarters
- 1 tbsp five-spice powder
- 1 tbsp soy sauce
- 1 tbsp hoisin sauce
- 1 tsp honey
- 1/2 tsp minced ginger
- Salt and black pepper, to taste

Preparation instructions:

1. Preheat the Air Fryer to 200°C for 5 minutes.
2. In a bowl, mix together the five-spice powder, soy sauce, hoisin sauce, honey, minced ginger, salt, and black pepper to make the marinade.
3. Coat the duck leg quarters with the marinade.
4. Place the duck legs in the air fryer basket.
5. Air fry at 200°C for about 40 minutes or until the duck is cooked through and the skin is crispy.

Air Fryer Sticky Sesame Chicken Wings

Serves 4

Prep Time 10 minutes / Cook Time 25 minutes

Ingredients:

- 500g chicken wings
- 2 tablespoons sesame oil

- 2 tablespoons soy sauce
- 2 tablespoons honey
- 1 tablespoon sesame seeds
- 2 spring onions, chopped

Preparation instructions:

1. In a large bowl, toss the chicken wings with the sesame oil, soy sauce, and honey.
2. Place the chicken wings in the air fryer basket.
3. Cook at 200°C for 25 minutes, shaking the basket halfway through, until the chicken wings are crispy and cooked through.
4. Sprinkle the cooked chicken wings with the sesame seeds and spring onions before serving.

Chicken Tenders

Serves: 4

Ingredients

- 500g chicken breast mini fillets
- 50g almond flour
- 50g grated parmesan cheese
- 1 tsp garlic powder
- 1 tsp onion powder
- 1 tsp smoked paprika
- 1/2 tsp salt
- 1/4 tsp black pepper
- 2 large eggs, beaten

Preparation instructions:

1. Preheat air fryer to 200°C.
2. In a shallow dish, mix together almond flour, parmesan cheese, garlic powder, onion powder, smoked paprika, salt, and black pepper.
3. In another shallow dish, beat the eggs.
4. Dip each chicken mini fillet in the egg mixture, then coat with the almond flour mixture, pressing the coating onto the chicken to make sure it sticks.
5. Place the chicken tenders in a single layer in the air fryer basket. You may need to work

Mustard Herb Pork Tenderloin

Serves 5

Prep time: 5 minutes / Cook time: 25 minutes

Ingredients

- 60 ml mayonnaise
- 2 tablespoons Dijon mustard
- ½ teaspoon dried thyme
- ¼ teaspoon dried rosemary
- 1 (450 g) pork tenderloin
- ½ teaspoon salt
- ¼ teaspoon ground black pepper

Preparation instructions

1. In a small bowl, mix mayonnaise, mustard, thyme, and rosemary. Brush tenderloin with mixture on all sides, then sprinkle with salt and pepper on all sides.
2. Place tenderloin into ungreased air fryer basket. Adjust the temperature to 204°C and air fry for 20 minutes, turning tenderloin halfway through cooking. Tenderloin will be golden and have an internal temperature of at least 64°C when done.
3. Serve warm.

Air Fryer Lamb Kofta Kebabs

Serves 4

Prep Time 20 minutes / Cook Time 10 minutes

Ingredients

- 500g ground lamb
- 1 onion, finely chopped
- 2 cloves garlic, minced
- 2 teaspoons ground cumin
- 2 teaspoons ground coriander
- Salt and pepper to taste

Preparation instructions

1. In a large bowl, mix together the ground lamb, onion, garlic, cumin, coriander, salt, and pepper.
2. Shape the mixture into long, thin kebabs around skewers.
3. Place the kebabs in the air fryer basket. Cook at 180°C for 10 minutes, turning halfway through, until the kebabs are browned and cooked through.

Chapter 7: Pizzas, Wraps, and Sandwiches

Margherita Mini Pizzas

Serves: 4
Prep time: 15 minutes / Cook time: 8 minutes

Ingredients:

- 4 mini pizza bases
- 200g mozzarella cheese, grated
- 1 large tomato, sliced
- Fresh basil leaves
- 2 tbsp olive oil
- Salt and black pepper, to taste

Preparation instructions:

1. Preheat the Air Fryer to 180°C for 5 minutes.
2. Place mini pizza bases in the air fryer basket.
3. Top each base with grated mozzarella and tomato slices.
4. Drizzle with olive oil and season with salt and black pepper.
5. Air fry at 180°C for about 8 minutes or until the cheese is melted and bubbly.
6. Garnish with fresh basil leaves before serving.

BBQ Chicken Flatbreads

Serves: 4
Prep time: 15 minutes / Cook time: 10 minutes

Ingredients:

- 2 cooked chicken breasts, shredded
- 4 flatbreads
- 120ml BBQ sauce
- 100g red onion, thinly sliced
- 100g cheddar cheese, grated
- Fresh coriander, chopped

Preparation instructions:

1. Preheat the Air Fryer to 180°C for 5 minutes.
2. In a bowl, mix shredded chicken with BBQ sauce.
3. Place flatbreads in the air fryer basket.
4. Spread the BBQ chicken mixture over the flatbreads.
5. Top with red onion slices and cheddar cheese.
6. Air fry at 180°C for about 10 minutes or until the cheese is melted.
7. Garnish with chopped coriander before serving.

Greek Gyro Wraps

Serves: 4
Prep time: 20 minutes / Cook time: 8 minutes

Ingredients:

- 400g gyro meat slices (chicken, beef, or lamb)
- 4 pita breads
- 150g Greek yoghurt
- 1 cucumber, diced
- 1 tomato, diced
- 1/2 red onion, thinly sliced
- Fresh dill, chopped
- Salt and black pepper, to taste

Preparation instructions:

1. Preheat the Air Fryer to 180°C for 5 minutes.
2. Place gyro meat slices in the air fryer basket.
3. Warm the pita bread in the air fryer for a few minutes.
4. In a bowl, mix Greek yoghurt with diced cucumber, chopped dill, salt, and black pepper.
5. Assemble the wraps with gyro meat, diced tomato, sliced red onion, and yoghurt sauce.
6. Air fry at 180°C for about 8 minutes or until the gyro meat is heated through.
7. Serve the Greek gyro wraps with fresh dill.

Caprese Panini

Serves: 4
Prep time: 15 minutes / Cook time: 6 minutes

Ingredients:

- 8 slices ciabatta or other bread
- 200g mozzarella cheese, sliced
- 2 large tomatoes, sliced
- Fresh basil leaves
- Balsamic glaze
- Olive oil, for brushing

Preparation instructions:

1. Preheat the Air Fryer to 180°C for 5 minutes.

2. Assemble sandwiches with mozzarella, tomato slices, and fresh basil leaves.
3. Drizzle balsamic glaze over the fillings.
4. Brush the outer sides of the sandwiches with olive oil.
5. Place sandwiches in the air fryer basket.
6. Air fry at 180°C for about 6 minutes or until the bread is toasted and the cheese is melted.
7. Drizzle more balsamic glaze before serving.

Buffalo Chicken Quesadillas

Serves: 4
Prep time: 15 minutes / Cook time: 8 minutes

Ingredients:
- 2 cooked chicken breasts, shredded
- 4 large flour tortillas
- 120ml buffalo sauce
- 100g cheddar cheese, grated
- 50g blue cheese, crumbled
- 2 green onions, sliced

Preparation instructions:
1. Preheat the Air Fryer to 180°C for 5 minutes.
2. In a bowl, mix shredded chicken with buffalo sauce.
3. Place a tortilla in the air fryer basket.
4. Spread the buffalo chicken mixture over half of the tortilla.
5. Top with cheddar cheese, blue cheese, and sliced green onions.
6. Fold the tortilla over the fillings to create a half-moon shape.
7. Air fry at 180°C for about 8 minutes or until the quesadilla is golden and crispy.
8. Repeat with remaining Ingredients.

Roast Veggie and Hummus Wraps

Serves: 4
Prep time: 20 minutes / Cook time: 12 minutes

Ingredients:
- 240g mixed vegetables (peppers, courgette, red onion), sliced
- 4 large whole wheat tortillas
- 120g hummus
- Fresh spinach leaves
- 2 tbsp olive oil
- 1 tsp dried oregano
- Salt and black pepper, to taste

Preparation instructions:
1. Preheat the Air Fryer to 180°C for 5 minutes.
2. In a bowl, toss mixed vegetables with olive oil, dried oregano, salt, and black pepper.
3. Place the vegetables in the air fryer basket.
4. Air fry at 180°C for about 12 minutes or until the vegetables are roasted and tender.
5. Warm the tortillas in the air fryer for a few minutes.
6. Spread hummus on each tortilla, add roasted vegetables, and top with fresh spinach.
7. Roll up the tortillas into wraps and serve.

Pesto Turkey and Cheese Panini

Serves: 4
Prep time: 15 minutes / Cook time: 6 minutes

Ingredients:
- 8 slices whole grain bread
- 300g cooked turkey slices
- 100g mozzarella cheese, sliced
- 60 ml pesto sauce
- Butter, for brushing

Preparation instructions:
1. Preheat the Air Fryer to 180°C for 5 minutes.
2. Assemble sandwiches with turkey slices, mozzarella cheese, and pesto sauce.
3. Butter the outer sides of the sandwiches.
4. Place sandwiches in the air fryer basket.
5. Air fry at 180°C for about 6 minutes or until the bread is toasted and the cheese is melted.
6. Serve the pesto turkey and cheese panini warm.

Hawaiian BBQ Pizza Pockets

Serves: 4
Prep time: 15 minutes / Cook time: 10 minutes

Ingredients:
- 4 whole wheat pizza dough pockets

- 200g cooked chicken, diced
- 100g pineapple chunks
- 120ml BBQ sauce
- 100g mozzarella cheese, shredded

Preparation instructions:

1. Preheat the Air Fryer to 180°C for 5 minutes.
2. In a bowl, mix diced chicken with BBQ sauce.
3. Fill each pizza dough pocket with chicken mixture, pineapple chunks, and mozzarella cheese.
4. Place the pizza pockets in the air fryer basket.
5. Air fry at 180°C for about 10 minutes or until the pockets are golden and the cheese is melted.
6. Serve the Hawaiian BBQ pizza pockets warm.

Philly Cheesesteak Sandwiches

Serves: 4
Prep time: 20 minutes / Cook time: 8 minutes

Ingredients:
- 2 cooked ribeye steaks, thinly sliced
- 2 large hoagie rolls
- 1 green pepper, sliced
- 1 onion, sliced
- 100g provolone cheese, sliced
- 2 tbsp olive oil
- Salt and black pepper, to taste

Preparation instructions:

1. Preheat the Air Fryer to 180°C for 5 minutes.
2. In a skillet, sauté sliced green pepper and onion in olive oil until tender. Season with salt and black pepper.
3. Fill each hoagie roll with sliced ribeye, sautéed pepper and onion mixture, and provolone cheese.
4. Place the sandwiches in the air fryer basket.
5. Air fry at 180°C for about 8 minutes or until the cheese is melted and bubbly.
6. Serve the Philly cheesesteak sandwiches warm.

Spicy Veggie Quesadillas

Serves: 4
Prep time: 15 minutes / Cook time: 8 minutes

Ingredients:
- 4 large flour tortillas
- 200g mixed peppers, sliced
- 1 jalapeño pepper, sliced
- 1 red onion, sliced
- 150g cheddar cheese, grated
- 2 tsp chilli powder
- 1/2 tsp cumin
- Salt and black pepper, to taste
- Olive oil, for brushing

Preparation instructions:

1. Preheat the Air Fryer to 180°C for 5 minutes.
2. In a bowl, toss mixed peppers, jalapeño pepper, and red onion with chilli powder, cumin, salt, and black pepper.
3. Place the vegetable mixture in the air fryer basket.
4. Air fry at 180°C for about 8 minutes or until the vegetables are tender and slightly charred. Place a tortilla in the air fryer basket.
5. Sprinkle grated cheddar cheese on half of the tortilla. Top with the spicy vegetable mixture and fold the tortilla over the fillings.
6. Brush the outer sides of the quesadilla with olive oil.
7. Air fry at 180°C for about 5 minutes or until the quesadilla is crispy and the cheese is melted.
8. Repeat with remaining Ingredients.

Mediterranean Chicken Pita Pockets

Serves: 4
Prep time: 20 minutes / Cook time: 10 minutes

Ingredients:
- 400g boneless chicken breast, sliced
- 4 whole wheat pita pockets
- 240g cherry tomatoes, halved
- 1/2 cucumber, diced
- 1/4 red onion, thinly sliced
- 100g feta cheese, crumbled
- Fresh parsley, chopped
- 2 tbsp olive oil
- 1 tbsp lemon juice
- 1 tsp dried oregano

- Salt and black pepper, to taste

Preparation instructions:

1. Preheat the Air Fryer to 180°C for 5 minutes.
2. In a bowl, marinate chicken slices with olive oil, lemon juice, dried oregano, salt, and black pepper.
3. Place the marinated chicken in the air fryer basket.
4. Air fry at 180°C for about 8-10 minutes or until the chicken is cooked through.
5. In a separate bowl, combine cherry tomatoes, cucumber, red onion, and crumbled feta.
6. Fill pita pockets with cooked chicken and the vegetable-feta mixture.
7. Garnish with chopped parsley before serving.

Meatball Marinara Subs

Serves: 4
Prep time: 20 minutes / Cook time: 10 minutes

Ingredients:

- 16 meatballs (beef, pork, or turkey)
- 4 sub rolls
- 200ml marinara sauce
- 100g mozzarella cheese, shredded
- Fresh basil leaves
- Olive oil, for brushing

Preparation instructions:

1. Preheat the Air Fryer to 180°C for 5 minutes.
2. Place meatballs in the air fryer basket.
3. Warm the sub rolls in the air fryer for a few minutes.
4. In a bowl, mix marinara sauce with shredded mozzarella.
5. Place meatballs in the sub rolls, pour marinara-cheese mixture over them.
6. Brush the outer sides of the subs with olive oil.
7. Air fry at 180°C for about 5 minutes or until the cheese is melted.
8. Garnish with fresh basil leaves before serving.

Spinach and Feta Calzones

Serves: 4
Prep time: 20 minutes / Cook time: 12 minutes

Ingredients:

- 4 store-bought pizza dough balls
- 200g frozen spinach, thawed and drained
- 150g feta cheese, crumbled
- 1/2 red onion, diced
- 1/2 tsp dried oregano
- 1/4 tsp crushed red pepper flakes
- Salt and black pepper, to taste
- Olive oil, for brushing

Preparation instructions:

1. Preheat the Air Fryer to 180°C for 5 minutes.
2. In a bowl, mix thawed spinach, crumbled feta, diced red onion, dried oregano, crushed red pepper flakes, salt, and black pepper.
3. Roll out each pizza dough ball into a circle.
4. Place a portion of the spinach-feta mixture on half of each dough circle.
5. Fold the other half of the dough over the filling to create a half-moon shape.
6. Seal the edges of the calzones by pressing with a fork.
7. Brush the calzones with olive oil. Place the calzones in the air fryer basket.
8. Air fry at 180°C for about 10-12 minutes or until the calzones are golden and crispy.
9. Serve the spinach and feta calzones warm.

Teriyaki Veggie Spring Rolls

Serves: 4
Prep time: 20 minutes / Cook time: 8 minutes

Ingredients:

- 8 rice paper spring roll wrappers
- 200g mixed vegetables (carrots, peppers, cucumber), julienned
- 100g rice vermicelli noodles, cooked and cooled
- 60ml teriyaki sauce
- Fresh coriander leaves
- Fresh mint leaves
- Sesame seeds, for garnish

Preparation instructions:

1. Preheat the Air Fryer to 180°C for 5 minutes.
2. Dip each rice paper wrapper in warm water for a few seconds to soften.
3. Lay the softened wrapper on a clean surface.

4. Place a small amount of julienned vegetables and cooked rice vermicelli on the wrapper.
5. Drizzle teriyaki sauce over the filling and top with fresh coriander and mint leaves.
6. Roll up the wrapper tightly, folding in the sides as you go.
7. Brush the spring rolls with a bit of water to seal the edges. Place the spring rolls in the air fryer basket.
8. Air fry at 180°C for about 6-8 minutes or until the spring rolls are crispy.
9. Garnish with sesame seeds before serving.

Turkey Avocado Club Wraps

Serves: 4
Prep time: 20 minutes / Cook time: 8 minutes

Ingredients:
- 4 large whole wheat tortillas
- 200g cooked turkey slices
- 1 avocado, sliced
- 8 slices bacon, cooked
- 1 tomato, sliced
- Fresh lettuce leaves
- Mayonnaise or ranch dressing, for spreading

Preparation instructions:
1. Preheat the Air Fryer to 180°C for 5 minutes.
2. Warm the tortillas in the air fryer for a few minutes.
3. Lay out a tortilla and spread a thin layer of mayonnaise or ranch dressing.
4. Place cooked turkey slices, avocado slices, bacon, tomato slices, and lettuce on the tortilla.
5. Roll up the tortilla tightly to form a wrap.
6. Place the wraps in the air fryer basket.
7. Air fry at 180°C for about 5-8 minutes or until the wraps are warm.
8. Serve the turkey avocado club wraps warm.

BBQ Pulled Jackfruit Sandwiches

Serves: 4
Prep time: 20 minutes / Cook time: 10 minutes

Ingredients:
- 400g canned young jackfruit, drained and shredded
- 4 burger buns
- 120ml BBQ sauce
- 1/2 red onion, thinly sliced
- Fresh coleslaw (cabbage and carrot mix)
- Olive oil, for sautéing
- Salt and black pepper, to taste

Preparation instructions:
1. Preheat the Air Fryer to 180°C for 5 minutes.
2. In a skillet, sauté shredded jackfruit with olive oil, salt, and black pepper until softened.
3. Add BBQ sauce to the jackfruit and cook for a few more minutes.
4. Warm the burger buns in the air fryer for a few minutes.
5. Assemble the sandwiches with pulled jackfruit, sliced red onion, and coleslaw.
6. Place the sandwiches in the air fryer basket.
7. Air fry at 180°C for about 5 minutes or until the sandwiches are warm.
8. Serve the BBQ pulled jackfruit sandwiches with extra coleslaw on the side.

Smoky Bacon and Egg Breakfast Pizzas

Serves: 4
Prep time: 15 minutes / Cook time: 8 minutes

Ingredients:
- 4 mini pizza crusts or flatbreads
- 4 large eggs
- 8 slices bacon, cooked and crumbled
- 100g cheddar cheese, grated
- 1/4 tsp smoked paprika
- Fresh chives, chopped
- Salt and black pepper, to taste

Preparation instructions:
1. Preheat the Air Fryer to 180°C for 5 minutes.
2. Place mini pizza crusts or flatbreads in the air fryer basket.
3. Crack an egg onto the centre of each crust.
4. Sprinkle grated cheddar cheese, crumbled bacon, smoked paprika, salt, and black pepper over the egg.

5. Air fry at 180°C for about 6-8 minutes or until the egg whites are set and the cheese is melted.
6. Garnish with chopped chives before serving.

Falafel and Tzatziki Flatbreads

Serves: 4

Prep time: 20 minutes / Cook time: 10 minutes

Ingredients:

- 4 flatbreads or pita breads
- 12 falafel balls
- 1/2 cucumber, diced
- 1/4 red onion, thinly sliced
- Fresh parsley, chopped
- 100g Greek yoghurt
- 1 clove garlic, minced
- 1 tbsp lemon juice
- 1/2 tsp dried dill
- Salt and black pepper, to taste

Preparation instructions:

1. Preheat the Air Fryer to 180°C for 5 minutes.
2. Warm the flatbreads in the air fryer for a few minutes.
3. In a bowl, mix Greek yoghurt, minced garlic, lemon juice, dried dill, salt, and black pepper to make tzatziki sauce.
4. Assemble the flatbreads with falafel balls, diced cucumber, sliced red onion, and chopped parsley.
5. Drizzle tzatziki sauce over the filling.
6. Place the assembled flatbreads in the air fryer basket.
7. Air fry at 180°C for about 5 minutes or until the falafel is heated through.
8. Serve the falafel and tzatziki flatbreads with extra sauce on the side.

Roast Beef and Cheddar Sliders

Serves: 4

Prep time: 20 minutes / Cook time: 8 minutes

Ingredients:

- 8 slider rolls
- 200g roast beef slices
- 100g cheddar cheese, sliced
- 60 ml mayonnaise
- 1 tbsp Dijon mustard
- 1 tbsp honey
- 1/2 tsp garlic powder
- Fresh arugula leaves

Preparation instructions:

1. Preheat the Air Fryer to 180°C for 5 minutes.
2. In a bowl, mix mayonnaise, Dijon mustard, honey, and garlic powder to make the sauce.
3. Split the slider rolls and spread the sauce on each side.
4. Place roast beef slices and cheddar cheese on the bottom half of the rolls.
5. Top with fresh arugula leaves and cover with the top half of the rolls.
6. Place the sliders in the air fryer basket.
7. Air fry at 180°C for about 5-8 minutes or until the cheese is melted and the sliders are warm.
8. Serve the roast beef and cheddar sliders warm.

Thai Peanut Chicken Wraps

Serves: 4

Prep time: 20 minutes / Cook time: 8 minutes

Ingredients:

- 4 large flour tortillas
- 2 cooked chicken breasts, sliced
- 120g shredded carrots
- 120g red cabbage, thinly sliced
- 60g chopped peanuts
- Fresh coriander leaves
- 60ml Thai peanut sauce

Preparation instructions:

1. Preheat the Air Fryer to 180°C for 5 minutes.
2. Warm the tortillas in the air fryer for a few minutes.
3. Lay out a tortilla and spread a thin layer of Thai peanut sauce.
4. Place sliced chicken, shredded carrots, red cabbage, chopped peanuts, and fresh coriander on the tortilla.
5. Roll up the tortilla tightly to form a wrap.
6. Place the wraps in the air fryer basket.
7. Air fry at 180°C for about 5-8 minutes or until the wraps are warm.
8. Serve the Thai peanut chicken wraps warm.

Air Fryer Grilled Caprese Sandwich

Serves: 4 people
Prep Time: 5 minutes / Cooking Time: 6-8 minutes

Ingredients:

- 2 large sub rolls, split lengthwise
- 200 g thinly sliced rib-eye beef
- 1 small onion, thinly sliced
- 1 red or green pepper, thinly sliced
- 2 cloves of garlic, minced
- 60 g grated cheddar cheese
- Salt and black pepper, to taste

Preparation instructions:

1. Preheat the air fryer to 400°F (200°C).
2. In a bowl, mix together the olive oil, salt, and pepper.
3. Brush each slice of bread with the olive oil mixture.
4. Layer a slice of bread with a slice of tomato, a slice of cheese, and two basil leaves.
5. Repeat the layering process with the other slice of bread on top.
6. Place the sandwich in the air fryer basket, making sure it is spaced evenly.
7. Air fry for 6-8 minutes, or until the bread is golden brown and the cheese is melted.
8. Serve hot and enjoy your delicious grilled Caprese sandwich.
9. Note: You can add some balsamic glaze to the sandwich for extra flavour.

Air Fryer BBQ Pulled Pork Wrap

Serves: 4 people
Prep Time: 10 minutes / Cooking Time: 1 hour 10 minutes

Ingredients:

- 700 g boneless pork shoulder, trimmed of excess fat
- 2 tsp salt
- 2 tsp paprika
- 1 tsp garlic powder
- 1 tsp onion powder
- 1 tsp black pepper
- 1 tsp dried thyme
- 2 tbsp tomato ketchup
- 1 tbsp apple cider vinegar
- 1 tbsp black treacle
- 4 large flour tortillas
- 200 g coleslaw
- 120 g barbecue sauce

Preparation instructions:

1. In a small bowl, mix together the salt, paprika, garlic powder, onion powder, black pepper, and thyme.
2. Rub the spice mix all over the pork shoulder and place it in the air fryer basket.
3. Cook at 180°C for 30 minutes, then turn the pork over and cook for another 30 minutes.
4. In a separate bowl, mix together the ketchup, vinegar, and black treacle to make the BBQ sauce.
5. Once the pork is cooked, remove it from the air fryer and use two forks to shred it into small pieces.
6. Place the shredded pork back into the air fryer and drizzle the BBQ sauce over it. Cook for a further 5-7 minutes, until the sauce is heated through and the pork is crispy.
7. While the pork is cooking, warm the tortillas in the air fryer for 1-2 minutes.
8. To assemble the wraps, place a tortilla on a plate, add a generous helping of coleslaw and a spoonful of the crispy BBQ pork. Roll up the wrap and serve immediately.

Air Fryer Veggie and Hummus Pita

Serves: 4 people
Prep Time: 10 minutes / Cooking Time: 6-8 minutes

Ingredients:
- 2 wholemeal pitas
- 100 g hummus
- 1 large carrot, grated
- 1 medium pepper, sliced
- 100 g cherry tomatoes, halved
- Salt, to taste
- Black pepper, to taste

Preparation instructions:
1. Preheat the air fryer to 200°C.
2. Cut each pita in half and spread a generous amount of hummus inside each half.
3. Fill each pita half with equal portions of grated carrot, sliced pepper, and halved cherry tomatoes.
4. Season with salt and black pepper to taste.
5. Place the stuffed pitas in the air fryer basket and cook for 6-8 minutes or until the pita is crispy and the veggies are slightly roasted.
6. Serve warm and enjoy!

Air Fryer Philly Cheesesteak Sandwich

Serves: 2 people
Prep Time: 10 minutes / Cooking Time: 10-15 minutes

Ingredients:
- 2 slices of bread of your choice
- 2 slices of tomato
- 2 slices of fresh mozzarella cheese
- 2 leaves of fresh basil
- 1 tablespoon olive oil
- Salt and pepper to taste

Preparation instructions:
1. Preheat the air fryer to 200°C.
2. In a pan over medium heat, cook the onions, peppers, and garlic until softened, about 5 minutes. Set aside.
3. Season the sliced beef with salt and pepper to taste.
4. Spread the sliced beef on the bottom half of the sub rolls.
5. Spoon the cooked onions, peppers, and garlic mixture over the beef.
6. Sprinkle the grated cheddar cheese over the vegetables.
7. Place the top half of the sub rolls on top of the cheese.
8. Place the filled sub rolls in the air fryer basket and cook for 6-8 minutes or until the cheese is melted and the bread is crispy.
9. Serve hot and enjoy your delicious Air Fryer Philly Cheesesteak Sandwich.

Crispy Parmesan Courgette Fries

Serves: 4
Prep time: 15 minutes / Cook time: 12 minutes

Ingredients:

- 2 medium courgettes, cut into fries
- 60g grated Parmesan cheese
- 60g breadcrumbs
- 1 tsp garlic powder
- 1/2 tsp paprika
- Salt and black pepper, to taste
- 1 large egg
- Cooking spray

Preparation instructions:

1. Preheat the Air Fryer to 200°C for 5 minutes.
2. In a bowl, mix grated Parmesan cheese, breadcrumbs, garlic powder, paprika, salt, and black pepper.
3. In another bowl, whisk the egg.
4. Dip courgette fries in the egg, then coat with the breadcrumb mixture.
5. Place the coated courgette fries in the air fryer basket in a single layer.
6. Lightly spray the fries with cooking spray.
7. Air fry at 200°C for about 10-12 minutes or until the fries are golden and crispy.
8. Serve the crispy Parmesan courgette fries with your favourite dip.

Loaded Potato Skins

Serves: 4
Prep time: 15 minutes / Cook time: 20 minutes

Ingredients:

- 4 large russet potatoes
- 100g shredded cheddar cheese
- 4 slices cooked bacon, crumbled
- 2 tbsp sour cream
- 2 tbsp chopped chives
- Salt and black pepper, to taste

Preparation instructions:

1. Preheat the Air Fryer to 200°C for 5 minutes.
2. Wash and dry potatoes, then prick them with a fork.
3. Air fry the potatoes at 200°C for about 20 minutes or until they are cooked through.
4. Cut each potato in half lengthwise and scoop out the flesh, leaving a thin layer.
5. Mix the potato flesh with shredded cheddar cheese, crumbled bacon, sour cream, chopped chives, salt, and black pepper.
6. Fill the potato skins with the mixture.
7. Place the loaded potato skins in the air fryer basket.
8. Air fry at 200°C for about 5-7 minutes or until the cheese is melted and the tops are crispy.
9. Serve the loaded potato skins warm.

Spinach and Artichoke Dip Stuffed Mushrooms

Serves: 4
Prep time: 20 minutes / Cook time: 10 minutes

Ingredients:

- 16 large button mushrooms, stems removed
- 100g frozen spinach, thawed and drained
- 100g canned artichoke hearts, chopped
- 60g cream cheese
- 60g shredded mozzarella cheese
- 2 tbsp grated Parmesan cheese
- 1 clove garlic, minced
- Salt and black pepper, to taste

Preparation instructions:

1. Preheat the Air Fryer to 180°C for 5 minutes.
2. In a bowl, mix thawed spinach, chopped artichoke hearts, cream cheese, shredded mozzarella cheese, grated Parmesan cheese, minced garlic, salt, and black pepper.
3. Fill each mushroom cap with the spinach-artichoke mixture.
4. Place the stuffed mushrooms in the air fryer

basket.

5. Air fry at 180°C for about 8-10 minutes or until the mushrooms are tender and the filling is heated through.

6. Serve the spinach and artichoke dip stuffed mushrooms warm.

Garlic Knots with Marinara

Serves: 4
Prep time: 20 minutes / Cook time: 10 minutes

Ingredients:
- 1 package refrigerated pizza dough
- 2 tbsp butter, melted
- 2 cloves garlic, minced
- 1 tbsp chopped fresh parsley
- Salt, to taste
- Marinara sauce, for dipping

Preparation instructions:
1. Preheat the Air Fryer to 180°C for 5 minutes.
2. Roll out the pizza dough and cut it into strips.
3. Tie each strip into a knot and place on a plate.
4. Mix melted butter, minced garlic, chopped parsley, and a pinch of salt.
5. Brush the garlic-butter mixture over the knots.
6. Place the garlic knots in the air fryer basket in a single layer.
7. Air fry at 180°C for about 8-10 minutes or until the knots are golden and cooked through.
8. Serve the garlic knots with marinara sauce for dipping.

Onion Rings with Creamy Dip

Serves: 4
Prep time: 15 minutes / Cook time: 10 minutes

Ingredients:
- 2 large onions, sliced into rings
- 100g all-purpose flour
- 1 tsp paprika
- 1/2 tsp garlic powder
- Salt and black pepper, to taste
- 1 large egg
- 120ml milk
- Cooking spray
- 60ml mayonnaise
- 1 tbsp ketchup
- 1 tsp Worcestershire sauce

Preparation instructions:
1. Preheat the Air Fryer to 200°C for 5 minutes.
2. In a bowl, mix flour, paprika, garlic powder, salt, and black pepper.
3. In another bowl, whisk the egg and milk.
4. Dip onion rings in the flour mixture, then into the egg mixture, and again in the flour mixture.
5. Place the coated onion rings in the air fryer basket in a single layer.
6. Lightly spray the onion rings with cooking spray.
7. Air fry at 200°C for about 8-10 minutes or until the onion rings are golden and crispy.
8. In a small bowl, mix mayonnaise, ketchup, and Worcestershire sauce to make the creamy dip.
9. Serve the onion rings with the creamy dip.

Sweet Potato Croquettes

Serves: 4
Prep time: 20 minutes / Cook time: 12 minutes

Ingredients:
- 2 large sweet potatoes, boiled and mashed
- 60g breadcrumbs
- 60g grated Parmesan cheese
- 1/2 tsp ground cumin
- 1/2 tsp smoked paprika
- Salt and black pepper, to taste
- 1 large egg
- Cooking spray

Preparation instructions:
1. Preheat the Air Fryer to 180°C for 5 minutes.
2. In a bowl, mix mashed sweet potatoes, breadcrumbs, grated Parmesan cheese, ground cumin, smoked paprika, salt, and black pepper.
3. Shape the mixture into croquettes.
4. In another bowl, whisk the egg.
5. Dip each croquette in the egg, then coat with breadcrumbs.
6. Place the coated croquettes in the air fryer

basket.

7. Lightly spray the croquettes with cooking spray.
8. Air fry at 180°C for about 10-12 minutes or until the croquettes are crispy and golden.
9. Serve the sweet potato croquettes with your favourite dipping sauce.

Crispy Coconut Onion Bites

Serves: 4
Prep time: 20 minutes / Cook time: 10 minutes

Ingredients:

- 2 large onions, sliced into rings
- 60g all-purpose flour
- 1/2 tsp curry powder
- 1/2 tsp turmeric powder
- Salt and black pepper, to taste
- 1 large egg
- 120ml coconut milk
- 100g shredded coconut
- Cooking spray
- Sweet chilli sauce, for dipping

Preparation instructions:

1. Preheat the Air Fryer to 200°C for 5 minutes.
2. In a bowl, mix flour, curry powder, turmeric powder, salt, and black pepper.
3. In another bowl, whisk the egg and coconut milk.
4. Dip onion rings in the flour mixture, then into the egg mixture, and finally coat with shredded coconut.
5. Place the coated onion rings in the air fryer basket in a single layer.
6. Lightly spray the onion rings with cooking spray.
7. Air fry at 200°C for about 8-10 minutes or until the coconut coating is golden and crispy.
8. Serve the crispy coconut onion bites with sweet chilli sauce for dipping.

Mini Cornbread Muffins

Serves: 4
Prep time: 15 minutes / Cook time: 12 minutes

Ingredients:

- 150g cornmeal
- 100g all-purpose flour
- 2 tsp baking powder
- 1/2 tsp salt
- 1 large egg
- 240 ml milk
- 2 tbsp melted butter
- 2 tbsp honey

Preparation instructions:

1. Preheat the Air Fryer to 180°C for 5 minutes.
2. In a bowl, mix cornmeal, all-purpose flour, baking powder, and salt.
3. In another bowl, whisk the egg, milk, melted butter, and honey.
4. Combine the wet and dry Ingredients to make the cornbread batter.
5. Grease a mini muffin tin or use silicone muffin cups.
6. Fill each muffin cup with the batter.
7. Place the muffin tin or cups in the air fryer basket.
8. Air fry at 180°C for about 10-12 minutes or until the cornbread muffins are golden and cooked through.
9. Serve the mini cornbread muffins warm.

Buffalo Cauliflower Bites

Serves: 4
Prep time: 20 minutes / Cook time: 15 minutes

Ingredients:

- 1 head cauliflower, cut into florets
- 60g all-purpose flour
- 1/2 tsp garlic powder
- 1/2 tsp onion powder
- 1/4 tsp paprika
- Salt and black pepper, to taste
- 120ml milk
- 60ml buffalo sauce
- 1 tbsp melted butter
- Ranch or blue cheese dressing, for dipping

Preparation instructions:

1. Preheat the Air Fryer to 180°C for 5 minutes.

2. In a bowl, mix flour, garlic powder, onion powder, paprika, salt, and black pepper.
3. In another bowl, whisk the milk and buffalo sauce.
4. Dip cauliflower florets in the milk-buffalo mixture, then into the flour mixture to coat.
5. Place the coated cauliflower florets in the air fryer basket in a single layer.
6. Lightly drizzle melted butter over the cauliflower.
7. Air fry at 180°C for about 12-15 minutes or until the cauliflower is crispy and cooked through.
8. Serve the buffalo cauliflower bites with ranch or blue cheese dressing for dipping.

Cheesy Spinach Stuffed Peppers

Serves: 4
Prep time: 15 minutes / Cook time: 15 minutes

Ingredients:
- 4 large peppers, halved and seeds removed
- 150g cooked spinach, chopped
- 100g cooked quinoa
- 100g shredded cheddar cheese
- 60g cream cheese
- 1/2 tsp garlic powder
- Salt and black pepper, to taste

Preparation instructions:
1. Preheat the Air Fryer to 180°C for 5 minutes.
2. In a bowl, mix cooked spinach, cooked quinoa, shredded cheddar cheese, cream cheese, garlic powder, salt, and black pepper.
3. Fill each pepper half with the spinach-quinoa mixture.
4. Place the stuffed peppers in the air fryer basket.
5. Air fry at 180°C for about 12-15 minutes or until the peppers are tender and the filling is heated through.
6. Serve the cheesy spinach stuffed peppers warm.

Mozzarella Stick Skewers

Serves: 4
Prep time: 15 minutes / Cook time: 8 minutes

Ingredients:
- 200g mozzarella cheese, cut into sticks
- 60g all-purpose flour
- 1 large egg
- 60g breadcrumbs
- 1/2 tsp Italian seasoning
- Marinara sauce, for dipping

Preparation instructions:
1. Preheat the Air Fryer to 200°C for 5 minutes.
2. Place flour, beaten egg, and breadcrumbs in separate bowls.
3. Dip each mozzarella stick in flour, then in the beaten egg, and finally coat with breadcrumbs mixed with Italian seasoning.
4. Thread the coated mozzarella sticks onto skewers.
5. Place the mozzarella stick skewers in the air fryer basket in a single layer.
6. Air fry at 200°C for about 6-8 minutes or until the mozzarella sticks are golden and the cheese is melted.
7. Serve the mozzarella stick skewers with marinara sauce for dipping.

Roasted Red Pepper Hummus

Serves: 4
Prep time: 10 minutes / Cook time: 5 minutes

Ingredients:
- 1 can (400g) chickpeas, drained and rinsed
- 2 roasted red peppers, peeled and seeded
- 2 tbsp tahini
- 2 cloves garlic, minced
- 2 tbsp lemon juice
- 2 tbsp olive oil
- 1/2 tsp cumin
- Salt and black pepper, to taste
- Fresh parsley, for garnish

Preparation instructions:
1. Preheat the Air Fryer to 180°C for 5 minutes.
2. In a food processor, blend chickpeas, roasted red peppers, tahini, minced garlic, lemon juice, olive oil, cumin, salt, and black pepper until smooth.
3. Transfer the hummus to a serving bowl and

garnish with fresh parsley.

4. Air fry at 180°C for 5 minutes.

5. Serve the roasted red pepper hummus with pita bread or vegetable sticks.

Crispy Garlic Herb Potatoes

Serves: 4

Prep time: 15 minutes / Cook time: 20 minutes

Ingredients:

- 500g baby potatoes, halved
- 2 tbsp olive oil
- 2 cloves garlic, minced
- 1 tsp dried thyme
- 1 tsp dried rosemary
- Salt and black pepper, to taste
- Fresh parsley, chopped, for garnish

Preparation instructions:

1. Preheat the Air Fryer to 180°C for 5 minutes.

2. In a bowl, toss halved baby potatoes with olive oil, minced garlic, dried thyme, dried rosemary, salt, and black pepper.

3. Place the seasoned potatoes in the air fryer basket.

4. Air fry at 180°C for about 18-20 minutes or until the potatoes are crispy and cooked through.

5. Garnish the crispy garlic herb potatoes with fresh chopped parsley.

6. Serve the potatoes as a side dish.

Teriyaki Glazed Brussels Sprouts

Serves: 4

Prep time: 10 minutes / Cook time: 15 minutes

Ingredients:

- 400g Brussels sprouts, halved
- 60ml teriyaki sauce
- 2 tbsp soy sauce
- 1 tbsp honey
- 1 tsp sesame oil
- Sesame seeds, for garnish
- Sliced green onions, for garnish

Preparation instructions:

1. Preheat the Air Fryer to 180°C for 5 minutes.

2. In a bowl, whisk teriyaki sauce, soy sauce, honey, and sesame oil.

3. Toss halved Brussels sprouts in the teriyaki mixture.

4. Place the Brussels sprouts in the air fryer basket.

5. Air fry at 180°C for about 12-15 minutes or until the Brussels sprouts are tender and caramelised.

6. Garnish the teriyaki glazed Brussels sprouts with sesame seeds and sliced green onions.

7. Serve the Brussels sprouts as a tasty side dish.

Caprese Salad Skewers

Serves: 4

Prep time: 15 minutes / Cook time: 5 minutes

Ingredients:

- 200g cherry tomatoes
- 200g fresh mozzarella balls
- Fresh basil leaves
- Balsamic glaze, for drizzling
- Salt and black pepper, to taste

Preparation instructions:

1. Preheat the Air Fryer to 180°C for 5 minutes.

2. Thread cherry tomatoes, fresh mozzarella balls, and fresh basil leaves onto small skewers.

3. Place the skewers in the air fryer basket in a single layer.

4. Air fry at 180°C for about 4-5 minutes or until the mozzarella begins to melt.

5. Drizzle the Caprese salad skewers with balsamic glaze.

6. Season with salt and black pepper to taste.

7. Serve the skewers as a delightful appetiser.

Jalapeno Popper Wontons

Serves: 4

Prep time: 20 minutes / Cook time: 10 minutes

Ingredients:

- 8 wonton wrappers
- 100g cream cheese, softened
- 50g shredded cheddar cheese
- 2 jalapeno peppers, seeded and finely chopped
- 1/2 tsp garlic powder

- Salt and black pepper, to taste
- Cooking spray
- Sour cream, for dipping

Preparation instructions:

1. Preheat the Air Fryer to 180°C for 5 minutes.
2. In a bowl, mix cream cheese, shredded cheddar cheese, chopped jalapeno peppers, garlic powder, salt, and black pepper.
3. Place a spoonful of the cream cheese mixture in the centre of each wonton wrapper.
4. Wet the edges of the wrapper with water, then fold diagonally to form triangles. Press to seal.
5. Lightly spray the wontons with cooking spray.
6. Place the wontons in the air fryer basket in a single layer.
7. Air fry at 180°C for about 8-10 minutes or until the wontons are golden and crispy.
8. Serve the jalapeno popper wontons with sour cream for dipping.

Creamy Mac 'n' Cheese Bites

Serves: 4
Prep time: 20 minutes / Cook time: 10 minutes

Ingredients:

- 200g macaroni pasta, cooked and drained
- 100g shredded cheddar cheese
- 60ml milk
- 2 tbsp cream cheese
- 1/2 tsp mustard powder
- 1/4 tsp garlic powder
- Salt and black pepper, to taste
- 1 large egg, beaten
- 60g breadcrumbs

Preparation instructions:

1. Preheat the Air Fryer to 180°C for 5 minutes.
2. In a saucepan, melt shredded cheddar cheese, milk, cream cheese, mustard powder, garlic powder, salt, and black pepper. Stir until smooth.
3. Combine the cooked macaroni pasta with the cheese sauce.
4. Allow the mixture to cool slightly, then stir in

the beaten egg.
5. Shape the mac 'n' cheese mixture into bite-sized balls.
6. Roll each ball in breadcrumbs to coat.
7. Place the mac 'n' cheese bites in the air fryer basket in a single layer.
8. Air fry at 180°C for about 8-10 minutes or until the bites are golden and crispy.
9. Serve the creamy mac 'n' cheese bites as a delightful snack or appetiser.

Mediterranean Quinoa Salad

Serves: 4
Prep time: 15 minutes / Cook time: 15 minutes

Ingredients:

- 200g cooked quinoa
- 1 cucumber, diced
- 200g cherry tomatoes, halved
- 1 red onion, finely chopped
- 100g feta cheese, crumbled
- 60g black olives, pitted and sliced
- 2 tbsp olive oil
- 2 tbsp lemon juice
- 1 tsp dried oregano
- Salt and black pepper, to taste
- Fresh parsley, chopped, for garnish

Preparation instructions:

1. Preheat the Air Fryer to 180°C for 5 minutes.
2. In a bowl, combine cooked quinoa, diced cucumber, cherry tomatoes, finely chopped red onion, crumbled feta cheese, and sliced black olives.
3. In a separate bowl, whisk together olive oil, lemon juice, dried oregano, salt, and black pepper to make the dressing.
4. Pour the dressing over the quinoa salad and toss to combine.
5. Air fry at 180°C for about 8-10 minutes or until the cheese is melted.
6. Garnish the Mediterranean quinoa salad with fresh chopped parsley.
7. Serve the salad as a refreshing side dish.

FRIED SHRIMP

Serves 4
Prep time: 25 minutes / Cook time: 30 minutes

Ingredients:

- 450g shrimp, peeled and deveined
- 120g all-purpose flour
- 2 eggs
- 240g bread crumbs
- Salt, to taste
- Ground black pepper, to taste
- Cooking spray
- 120g mayonnaise
- 2 tbsp whole-grain mustard
- 2 tbsp chopped pickled jalapenos
- 1 tbsp hot sauce
- 1 tbsp ketchup
- 1 scallion, sliced

Preparation instructions:

1. Pat dry the shrimp using paper towels, and season with salt and pepper.
2. Whisk flour with ¾ teaspoon of salt and some pepper in a bowl. Whisk eggs and ¼ tsp of salt in a separate bowl. Pour the bread crumbs into a third bowl.
3. Dip the shrimp in the flour, shake off the excess, and dip in the beaten eggs. Let the excess drip off, and dredge in the bread crumbs. Transfer the coated shrimp to a baking sheet.
4. Preheat the air fryer to 385 degrees.
5. In batches, arrange the shrimp in a single layer in the air fryer basket. Spritz with cooking spray, and cook for 10 minutes until golden brown, flipping halfway through the cooking.
6. Stir the mayonnaise, mustard, ketchup, hot sauce, pickled jalapenos and scallion in a bowl until smooth.
7. Serve the fried sauce with the dipping sauce.

GARLIC BREAD

Serves 8
Prep time: 10 minutes / Cook time: 10 minutes

Ingredients:

- 8 slices French bread
- 60g butter, softened
- 3 tbsp grated Parmesan cheese
- 2 cloves garlic, minced
- 2 tsp minced fresh parsley

Preparation instructions:

1. Preheat the air fryer to 350 degrees.
2. Combine the butter, Parmesan, garlic and parsley in a bowl, and spread over the bread slices.
3. In batches, arrange the bread in a single layer on the tray in the air fryer basket. Cook for about 5 minutes until golden brown.
4. Serve warm.

Chapter 9: Vegan and Veggie

Chickpea and Spinach Curry

Serves: 4
Prep time: 15 minutes / Cook time: 20 minutes

Ingredients:
- 400g canned chickpeas, drained and rinsed
- 200g fresh spinach leaves
- 1 onion, finely chopped
- 2 cloves garlic, minced
- 1 tsp ginger, minced
- 1 tsp curry powder
- 1/2 tsp ground turmeric
- 1/2 tsp ground cumin
- 1/2 tsp ground coriander
- 400ml coconut milk
- 200ml vegetable broth
- 2 tbsp olive oil
- Salt and black pepper, to taste

Preparation instructions:
1. Preheat the Air Fryer to 180°C for 5 minutes.
2. In a pan, heat olive oil and sauté the chopped onion until translucent.
3. Add minced garlic and ginger, and cook for another minute.
4. Stir in curry powder, ground turmeric, ground cumin, and ground coriander.
5. Add canned chickpeas, coconut milk, and vegetable broth. Simmer for about 10 minutes.
6. Add fresh spinach leaves and cook until wilted.
7. Air Fryer to 180°C for 5 minutes.
8. Season with salt and black pepper.
9. Serve the chickpea and spinach curry over rice or with naan bread.

Crispy Tofu Bites with Sweet chilli Sauce

Serves: 4
Prep time: 20 minutes / Cook time: 15 minutes

Ingredients:
- 300g firm tofu, cubed
- 60g cornstarch
- 1/2 tsp garlic powder
- 1/2 tsp onion powder
- 1/4 tsp paprika
- Salt and black pepper, to taste
- Cooking spray
- 100ml sweet chilli sauce

Preparation instructions:
1. Preheat the Air Fryer to 200°C for 5 minutes.
2. In a bowl, mix cornstarch, garlic powder, onion powder, paprika, salt, and black pepper.
3. Toss tofu cubes in the cornstarch mixture to coat.
4. Lightly spray the coated tofu cubes with cooking spray.
5. Place the tofu cubes in the air fryer basket in a single layer.
6. Air fry at 200°C for about 12-15 minutes or until the tofu is crispy and golden.
7. Serve the crispy tofu bites with sweet chilli sauce for dipping.

Veggie-Stuffed peppers

Serves: 4
Prep time: 20 minutes / Cook time: 20 minutes

Ingredients:
- 4 peppers, halved and seeds removed
- 200g cooked quinoa
- 150g mixed vegetables (such as corn, peas, and carrots)
- 1 onion, finely chopped
- 2 cloves garlic, minced
- 200ml tomato sauce
- 1 tsp dried oregano
- 1 tsp dried basil
- Salt and black pepper, to taste
- Olive oil, for sautéing

Preparation instructions:
1. Preheat the Air Fryer to 180°C for 5 minutes.

2. In a pan, sauté chopped onion and minced garlic in olive oil until translucent.

3. Add mixed vegetables and cook until tender.

4. Stir in cooked quinoa, tomato sauce, dried oregano, dried basil, salt, and black pepper.

5. Fill each pepper half with the quinoa-vegetable mixture.

6. Place the stuffed peppers in the air fryer basket.

7. Air fry at 180°C for about 18-20 minutes or until the peppers are tender.

8. Serve the veggie-stuffed peppers as a wholesome meal.

Lentil and Mushroom Shepherd's Pie

Serves: 4
Prep time: 20 minutes / Cook time: 20 minutes

Ingredients:

- 300g cooked green lentils
- 200g mushrooms, chopped
- 1 onion, finely chopped
- 2 cloves garlic, minced
- 200ml vegetable broth
- 1 tsp tomato paste
- 1 tsp thyme
- 1 tsp rosemary
- 400g mashed potatoes
- Salt and black pepper, to taste
- Olive oil, for sautéing

Preparation instructions:

1. Preheat the Air Fryer to 180°C for 5 minutes.

2. In a pan, sauté chopped onion and minced garlic in olive oil until translucent.

3. Add chopped mushrooms and cook until they release moisture.

4. Stir in cooked green lentils, vegetable broth, tomato paste, thyme, and rosemary.

5. Simmer until the mixture thickens. Season with salt and black pepper.

6. Divide the lentil and mushroom mixture into individual ramekins. Top with mashed potatoes. Place the ramekins in the air fryer basket.

7. Air fry at 180°C for about 15-20 minutes or until the mashed potatoes are golden and crispy.

8. Serve the lentil and mushroom shepherd's pie as a comforting vegan dish.

Vegan Buffalo Cauliflower Tacos

Serves: 4
Prep time: 20 minutes / Cook time: 20 minutes

Ingredients:

- 1 small head cauliflower, cut into florets
- 60ml buffalo sauce
- 60ml almond milk
- 60g chickpea flour
- 1 tsp garlic powder
- 1 tsp onion powder
- 1/2 tsp paprika
- Salt and black pepper, to taste
- 8 small soft tortillas
- Shredded lettuce, for topping
- Diced tomatoes, for topping
- Vegan ranch dressing, for drizzling

Preparation instructions:

1. Preheat the Air Fryer to 180°C for 5 minutes.

2. In a bowl, mix buffalo sauce and almond milk.

3. In another bowl, whisk chickpea flour, garlic powder, onion powder, paprika, salt, and black pepper.

4. Dip cauliflower florets in the buffalo sauce mixture, then coat with chickpea flour mixture.

5. Place the coated cauliflower florets in the air fryer basket.

6. Air fry at 180°C for about 15-20 minutes or until the cauliflower is crispy and golden.

7. Warm the tortillas.

8. Assemble the tacos by placing crispy buffalo cauliflower in tortillas.

9. Top with shredded lettuce, diced tomatoes, and drizzle with vegan ranch dressing.

Mediterranean Stuffed Aubergine

Serves: 4
Prep time: 20 minutes / Cook time: 25 minutes

Ingredients:
- 2 aubergines
- 200g cooked quinoa
- 100g cherry tomatoes, halved
- 60g Kalamata olives, pitted and sliced
- 60g red onion, finely chopped
- 60g fresh parsley, chopped
- 2 tbsp olive oil
- 2 tbsp lemon juice
- 1 tsp dried oregano
- Salt and black pepper, to taste

Preparation instructions:
1. Preheat the Air Fryer to 180°C for 5 minutes.
2. Cut aubergines in half lengthwise and scoop out the flesh, leaving a shell.
3. Dice the aubergine flesh and sauté in olive oil until softened.
4. In a bowl, mix cooked quinoa, sautéed aubergine, cherry tomatoes, Kalamata olives, red onion, and fresh parsley.
5. In a separate bowl, whisk olive oil, lemon juice, dried oregano, salt, and black pepper to make the dressing.
6. Combine the dressing with the quinoa mixture.
7. Fill the aubergine shells with the quinoa mixture. Place the stuffed aubergines in the air fryer basket.
8. Air fry at 180°C for about 20-25 minutes or until the aubergine is tender.
9. Serve the Mediterranean stuffed aubergine as a delightful vegan dish.

Spicy Black Bean Burger Sliders

Serves: 4
Prep time: 20 minutes / Cook time: 20 minutes

Ingredients:
- 400g canned black beans, drained and rinsed
- 50g breadcrumbs
- 60g red onion, finely chopped
- 2 cloves garlic, minced
- 1 tsp chilli powder
- 1/2 tsp cumin
- 1/2 tsp paprika
- Salt and black pepper, to taste
- 8 mini burger buns
- Lettuce, tomato slices, and red onion slices, for topping
- Vegan mayo or sauce of choice, for spreading

Preparation instructions:
1. Preheat the Air Fryer to 180°C for 5 minutes.
2. In a bowl, mash black beans with a fork or potato masher.
3. Add breadcrumbs, finely chopped red onion, minced garlic, chilli powder, cumin, paprika, salt, and black pepper.
4. Mix well and shape the mixture into mini burger patties.
5. Place the black bean burger patties in the air fryer basket.
6. Air fry at 180°C for about 15-20 minutes or until the patties are crispy and heated through.
7. Warm the mini burger buns.
8. Assemble the sliders by placing black bean burger patties on the buns.
9. Top with lettuce, tomato slices, red onion slices, and spread vegan mayo or sauce of choice.

Teriyaki Tempeh Skewers

Serves: 4
Prep time: 15 minutes / Cook time: 15 minutes

Ingredients:
- 200g tempeh, cubed
- 60ml teriyaki sauce
- 2 tbsp soy sauce
- 2 tbsp maple syrup
- 1 tsp sesame oil
- 1 tsp minced ginger

- 1 tsp minced garlic
- 1 red pepper, cut into chunks
- 1 green pepper, cut into chunks
- 1 red onion, cut into chunks
- Wooden skewers, soaked in water

Preparation instructions:

1. Preheat the Air Fryer to 180°C for 5 minutes.
2. In a bowl, mix teriyaki sauce, soy sauce, maple syrup, sesame oil, minced ginger, and minced garlic.
3. Add cubed tempeh to the marinade and let it marinate for about 10 minutes.
4. Thread marinated tempeh cubes, pepper chunks, and onion chunks onto the soaked wooden skewers.
5. Place the skewers in the air fryer basket.
6. Air fry at 180°C for about 12-15 minutes or until the tempeh and vegetables are cooked and slightly charred.
7. Serve the teriyaki tempeh skewers with rice or noodles.

Vegan Pesto Zoodles

Serves: 4
Prep time: 15 minutes / Cook time: 10 minutes

Ingredients:

- 4 medium courgettes, spiralized into zoodles
- 100g cherry tomatoes, halved
- 60 ml vegan pesto
- 2 tbsp nutritional yeast
- Salt and black pepper, to taste
- Fresh basil leaves, for garnish

Preparation instructions:

1. Preheat the Air Fryer to 180°C for 5 minutes.
2. In a bowl, toss zoodles with halved cherry tomatoes and vegan pesto.
3. Place the zoodle mixture in the air fryer basket.
4. Air fry at 180°C for about 8-10 minutes or until the zoodles are tender.
5. Season with nutritional yeast, salt, and black pepper.
6. Garnish with fresh basil leaves before serving.

Quinoa-Stuffed Acorn Squash

Serves: 4
Prep time: 20 minutes / Cook time: 40 minutes

Ingredients:

- 2 acorn squash, halved and seeds removed
- 200g cooked quinoa
- 100g baby spinach
- 60g dried cranberries
- 60g chopped pecans
- 1/4 tsp cinnamon
- 1/4 tsp nutmeg
- Salt and black pepper, to taste
- Olive oil, for drizzling

Preparation instructions:

1. Preheat the Air Fryer to 180°C for 5 minutes.
2. Drizzle olive oil over the cut sides of the acorn squash.
3. Place the acorn squash halves in the air fryer basket, cut side down.
4. Air fry at 180°C for about 15-20 minutes or until the squash is slightly tender.
5. In a bowl, mix cooked quinoa, baby spinach, dried cranberries, chopped pecans, cinnamon, nutmeg, salt, and black pepper.
6. Divide the quinoa mixture among the acorn squash halves.
7. Place the stuffed acorn squash halves in the air fryer basket, cut side up.
8. Air fry at 180°C for an additional 15-20 minutes or until the squash is fully cooked and the stuffing is heated through.
9. Serve the quinoa-stuffed acorn squash as a delightful fall-inspired dish.

Portobello Mushroom Steaks

Serves: 4
Prep time: 15 minutes / Cook time: 15 minutes

Ingredients:

- 4 large portobello mushrooms, stems removed
- 60ml balsamic vinegar
- 2 tbsp olive oil

- 2 cloves garlic, minced
- 1 tsp dried thyme
- Salt and black pepper, to taste
- Fresh parsley, for garnish

Preparation instructions:
1. Preheat the Air Fryer to 180°C for 5 minutes.
2. In a bowl, whisk together balsamic vinegar, olive oil, minced garlic, dried thyme, salt, and black pepper.
3. Brush the balsamic mixture over both sides of the portobello mushrooms.
4. Place the portobello mushrooms in the air fryer basket.
5. Air fry at 180°C for about 12-15 minutes or until the mushrooms are tender.
6. Garnish with fresh parsley before serving.

Cauliflower Chilli Bites

Serves: 4
Prep time: 15 minutes / Cook time: 20 minutes

Ingredients:
- 1 small head cauliflower, cut into florets
- 60ml chilli sauce
- 2 tbsp soy sauce
- 1 tbsp maple syrup
- 1 tsp sesame oil
- 1/2 tsp minced ginger
- 1/2 tsp minced garlic
- 1/4 tsp red pepper flakes (adjust to taste)
- Salt and black pepper, to taste

Preparation instructions:
1. Preheat the Air Fryer to 180°C for 5 minutes.
2. In a bowl, mix chilli sauce, soy sauce, maple syrup, sesame oil, minced ginger, minced garlic, red pepper flakes, salt, and black pepper.
3. Toss cauliflower florets in the chilli sauce mixture to coat.
4. Place the coated cauliflower florets in the air fryer basket.
5. Air fry at 180°C for about 18-20 minutes or until the cauliflower is crispy and cooked through.
6. Serve the cauliflower chilli bites as a spicy and flavorful appetisers.

Thai Peanut Noodle Stir-Fry

Serves: 4
Prep time: 15 minutes / Cook time: 15 minutes

Ingredients:
- 200g rice noodles, cooked according to package instructions
- 200g mixed vegetables (such as peppers, carrots, and snap peas), sliced
- 100g tofu, cubed
- 60ml peanut sauce
- 2 tbsp soy sauce
- 1 tbsp lime juice
- 1 tsp sesame oil
- 1/2 tsp minced garlic
- 1/4 tsp red pepper flakes (adjust to taste)
- Chopped peanuts and fresh coriander, for garnish

Preparation instructions:
1. Preheat the Air Fryer to 180°C for 5 minutes.
2. In a bowl, mix peanut sauce, soy sauce, lime juice, sesame oil, minced garlic, and red pepper flakes.
3. Toss cooked rice noodles, mixed vegetables, and cubed tofu in the sauce mixture.
4. Place the noodle and vegetable mixture in the air fryer basket.
5. Air fry at 180°C for about 10-12 minutes or until the tofu is heated and the vegetables are slightly crispy.
6. Garnish with chopped peanuts and fresh coriander before serving.

Vegan Spinach and Artichoke Dip

Serves: 4
Prep time: 10 minutes / Cook time: 15 minutes

Ingredients:
- 200g frozen chopped spinach, thawed and drained

- 150g canned artichoke hearts, chopped
- 120ml vegan cream cheese
- 60ml vegan mayonnaise
- 60ml unsweetened almond milk
- 2 cloves garlic, minced
- 2 tbsp nutritional yeast
- 1 tbsp lemon juice
- 1/2 tsp onion powder
- Salt and black pepper, to taste

Preparation instructions:
1. Preheat the Air Fryer to 180°C for 5 minutes.
2. In a bowl, mix chopped spinach, chopped artichoke hearts, vegan cream cheese, vegan mayonnaise, almond milk, minced garlic, nutritional yeast, lemon juice, onion powder, salt, and black pepper.
3. Transfer the mixture to an oven-safe dish that fits in the air fryer.
4. Air fry at 180°C for about 12-15 minutes or until the dip is heated through and slightly bubbly.
5. Serve the vegan spinach and artichoke dip with your favourite dippers.

Stuffed Sweet Potato Skins

Serves: 4
Prep time: 15 minutes / Cook time: 40 minutes

Ingredients:
- 2 medium sweet potatoes
- 200g cooked black beans
- 1/2 avocado, diced
- 60g diced red onion
- 60g diced pepper
- 40g chopped fresh coriander
- 1 tbsp lime juice
- 1 tsp ground cumin
- 1/2 tsp chilli powder
- Salt and black pepper, to taste

Preparation instructions:
1. Preheat the Air Fryer to 180°C for 5 minutes.
2. Wash sweet potatoes and pat dry. Prick the sweet potatoes with a fork.
3. Place the sweet potatoes in the air fryer basket.

4. Air fry at 180°C for about 35-40 minutes or until the sweet potatoes are tender.
5. While the sweet potatoes are cooking, in a bowl, mix cooked black beans, diced avocado, diced red onion, diced pepper, chopped coriander, lime juice, ground cumin, chilli powder, salt, and black pepper.
6. Once the sweet potatoes are cooked, cut them in half lengthwise and scoop out some of the flesh to create a hollow.
7. Fill the sweet potato skins with the black bean and avocado mixture.
8. Place the stuffed sweet potato skins in the air fryer basket. Air fry at 180°C for an additional 5-7 minutes to heat the filling.
9. Serve the stuffed sweet potato skins as a hearty and satisfying dish.

Mediterranean Chickpea Salad Wraps

Serves: 4
Prep time: 15 minutes / Cook time: 5 minutes

Ingredients:
- 400g canned chickpeas, drained and rinsed
- 150g diced cucumber
- 150g diced tomato
- 60g diced red onion
- 60g chopped Kalamata olives
- 40g chopped fresh parsley
- 2 tbsp extra-virgin olive oil
- 1 tbsp lemon juice
- 1 tsp dried oregano
- Salt and black pepper, to taste
- 4 whole wheat tortilla wraps

Preparation instructions:
1. In a bowl, mix canned chickpeas, diced cucumber, diced tomato, diced red onion, chopped Kalamata olives, chopped parsley, olive oil, lemon juice, dried oregano, salt, and black pepper.
2. Warm the whole wheat tortilla wraps slightly.
3. Place a generous amount of the Mediterranean

chickpea salad on each tortilla.

4. Wrap the tortillas, folding in the sides first and then rolling them up.

5. Air Fryer to 180°C for 5 minutes.

6. Serve the Mediterranean chickpea salad wraps as a fresh and flavorful lunch or dinner option.

Crispy Brussels Sprouts Toss

Serves: 4

Prep time: 10 minutes / Cook time: 20 minutes

Ingredients:

- 300g Brussels sprouts, trimmed and halved
- 2 tbsp olive oil
- 1 tbsp balsamic vinegar
- 1 tbsp maple syrup
- 1/2 tsp Dijon mustard
- Salt and black pepper, to taste
- 30g chopped walnuts
- 30g dried cranberries

Preparation instructions:

1. Preheat the Air Fryer to 180°C for 5 minutes.

2. In a bowl, mix olive oil, balsamic vinegar, maple syrup, Dijon mustard, salt, and black pepper.

3. Toss halved Brussels sprouts in the olive oil mixture to coat.

4. Place the coated Brussels sprouts in the air fryer basket.

5. Air fry at 180°C for about 18-20 minutes or until the Brussels sprouts are crispy and caramelised.

6. Toss the air-fried Brussels sprouts with chopped walnuts and dried cranberries.

7. Serve the crispy Brussels sprouts toss as a delightful side dish or salad.

Vegan Spring Rolls with Peanut Dipping Sauce

Serves: 4

Prep time: 20 minutes / Cook time: 10 minutes

Ingredients:

For the spring rolls:
- 8 rice paper wrappers
- 100g vermicelli rice noodles, cooked

according to package instructions
- 240g shredded lettuce
- 240g julienned carrots
- 240g julienned cucumber
- 40g fresh mint leaves
- 40g fresh coriander leaves

For the peanut dipping sauce:
- 60ml peanut butter
- 2 tbsp soy sauce
- 1 tbsp lime juice
- 1 tbsp maple syrup
- 1/2 tsp minced garlic
- 1/4 tsp minced ginger
- Water, as needed

Preparation instructions:

1. Prepare all the vegetables and herbs for the spring rolls.

2. Fill a large bowl with warm water.

3. Dip a rice paper wrapper into the warm water for a few seconds until it softens.

4. Place the softened rice paper wrapper on a clean surface.

5. Layer a small amount of cooked vermicelli rice noodles, shredded lettuce, julienned carrots, julienned cucumber, fresh mint leaves, and fresh coriander leaves on the lower half of the wrapper.

6. Fold the sides of the wrapper over the filling and then roll it up tightly.

7. Repeat the process to make the remaining spring rolls.

8. In a bowl, whisk together peanut butter, soy sauce, lime juice, maple syrup, minced garlic, and minced ginger. Add water as needed to achieve the desired dipping sauce consistency.

9. Air Fryer to 180°C for 5 minutes.

10.Serve the spring rolls with the peanut dipping sauce as a light and refreshing appetisers.

Tofu and Veggie Kebabs

Serves: 4

Prep time: 20 minutes / Cook time: 15 minutes

Ingredients:

* 200g extra-firm tofu, pressed and cubed
* 1 red pepper, cut into chunks
* 1 yellow pepper, cut into chunks
* 1 red onion, cut into chunks
* 120ml teriyaki sauce
* 1 tbsp sesame oil
* 1/2 tsp minced garlic
* 1/4 tsp minced ginger
* Wooden skewers, soaked in water

Preparation instructions:

1. Preheat the Air Fryer to 180°C for 5 minutes.
2. In a bowl, mix teriyaki sauce, sesame oil, minced garlic, and minced ginger.
3. Toss cubed tofu, pepper chunks, and red onion chunks in the teriyaki sauce mixture to coat.
4. Thread the marinated tofu and veggies onto the soaked wooden skewers.
5. Place the tofu and veggie skewers in the air fryer basket.
6. Air fry at 180°C for about 12-15 minutes or until the tofu is golden and the veggies are tender.
7. Serve the tofu and veggie kebabs as a flavorful and protein-rich dish.

Vegan Margherita Flatbreads

Serves: 4
Prep time: 15 minutes / Cook time: 12 minutes

Ingredients:

* 4 whole wheat flatbreads
* 200g vegan mozzarella cheese, shredded
* 2 large tomatoes, sliced
* Fresh basil leaves
* 2 tbsp extra-virgin olive oil
* 1/2 tsp dried oregano
* Salt and black pepper, to taste

Preparation instructions:

1. Preheat the Air Fryer to 180°C for 5 minutes.
2. Place the flatbreads on a clean surface.
3. Sprinkle a layer of shredded vegan mozzarella cheese on each flatbread.
4. Arrange tomato slices and fresh basil leaves over

the cheese.
5. Drizzle extra-virgin olive oil over the toppings and sprinkle with dried oregano, salt, and black pepper.
6. Transfer the flatbreads to the air fryer basket in batches if necessary.
7. Air fry at 180°C for about 8-10 minutes or until the cheese is melted and bubbly.
8. Serve the vegan Margherita flatbreads as a delightful and plant-based meal.

Roasted Veggie and Hummus Wraps

Serves: 4
Prep time: 15 minutes / Cook time: 20 minutes

Ingredients:

* 200g mixed vegetables (such as peppers, courgette, and red onion), sliced
* 2 tbsp olive oil
* 1 tsp dried thyme
* Salt and black pepper, to taste
* 4 whole wheat tortilla wraps
* 200g hummus
* Fresh baby spinach leaves

Preparation instructions:

1. Preheat the Air Fryer to 180°C for 5 minutes.
2. In a bowl, toss sliced mixed vegetables with olive oil, dried thyme, salt, and black pepper.
3. Place the coated mixed vegetables in the air fryer basket.
4. Air fry at 180°C for about 15-20 minutes or until the vegetables are roasted and tender.
5. Warm the whole wheat tortilla wraps slightly.
6. Spread a generous amount of hummus on each tortilla.
7. Layer roasted mixed vegetables and fresh baby spinach leaves on top of the hummus.
8. Wrap the tortillas, folding in the sides first and then rolling them up.
9. Serve the roasted veggie and hummus wraps as a wholesome and satisfying option.

Vegan Pesto and Tomato Crostini

Serves: 4

Prep time: 10 minutes / Cook time: 5 minutes

Ingredients:
- 4 slices of baguette or ciabatta bread
- 60g vegan pesto
- 2 large tomatoes, sliced
- Fresh basil leaves
- Salt and black pepper, to taste

Preparation instructions:
1. Preheat the Air Fryer to 180°C for 5 minutes.
2. Place the bread slices in the air fryer basket.
3. Air fry at 180°C for about 3-5 minutes or until the bread is toasted and golden.
4. Spread a layer of vegan pesto on each toasted bread slice.
5. Arrange tomato slices and fresh basil leaves over the pesto.
6. Sprinkle it with salt and black pepper to taste.
7. Serve the vegan pesto and tomato crostini as a flavorful and appetising snack.

Air Fryer Stuffed Artichokes

Serves 4

Prep Time 15 minutes / Cook Time 20 minutes
- Ingredients:
- 2 artichokes, halved and choke removed
- 2 tablespoons olive oil
- Salt and pepper to taste
- 50g breadcrumbs
- 50g grated Parmesan cheese

Preparation instructions:
1. Brush the artichokes with the olive oil and season with salt and pepper.
2. Mix the breadcrumbs and Parmesan cheese together and stuff into the artichoke halves.
3. Place the stuffed artichokes in the air fryer basket.
4. Cook at 180°C for 20 minutes, until the artichokes are tender and the topping is golden brown.

Air Fryer Crispy Tofu

Serves 4,

Cooking Time: 20 minutes

Ingredients:
- 400g firm tofu, drained and pressed
- 2 tbsp cornflour
- 1 tsp smoked paprika
- 1 tsp garlic powder
- 1/2 tsp salt
- 1/4 tsp black pepper
- Cooking spray

Preparation instructions:
1. Preheat the air fryer to 200°C.
2. Cut the tofu into small cubes.
3. In a small bowl, mix together the cornflour, smoked paprika, garlic powder, salt and black pepper.
4. Toss the tofu in the spice mixture until evenly coated.
5. Spray the air fryer basket with cooking spray.
6. Arrange the tofu in a single layer in the air fryer basket.
7. Cook for 10 minutes, then flip the tofu and cook for another 10 minutes until golden and crispy.
8. Serve hot with your favourite dipping sauce.

Air Fryer Sweet Potato Fries

Serves 4,

Cooking time: 20 minutes

Ingredients:
- 2 large sweet potatoes, peeled and cut into fries
- 2 tbsp olive oil
- 1 tsp garlic powder
- 1 tsp smoked paprika
- Salt and pepper to taste

Preparation instructions:
1. Preheat the air fryer to 200°C.
2. In a mixing bowl, combine sweet potato fries, olive oil, garlic powder, smoked paprika, salt, and pepper.

3. Toss the fries until they are well coated.
4. Place the fries in the air fryer basket in a single layer.
5. Cook for 15-20 minutes, shaking the basket halfway through, or until the fries are crispy and golden brown.

Nutritional Information per serving:
180 Calories, 8g Fat, 25g Carbohydrates, 3g Fibre, 2g Protein, 230mg Sodium, 4g Sugar.

Air Fryer Tofu Stir Fry with Vegetables

Serves: 4 people
Prep Time: 10 minutes / Cooking Time: 15-20 minutes

Ingredients
- 450 g extra firm tofu, drained and cut into bite-sized cubes
- 2 tbsp cornstarch
- 1 tsp salt
- 1 tsp black pepper
- 2 tbsp vegetable oil
- 2 bell peppers, sliced
- 1 onion, sliced
- 2 cloves of garlic, minced
- 200 g broccoli florets
- 2 tbsp soy sauce
- 2 tbsp hoisin sauce
- 1 tsp sesame oil

Preparation instructions
1. In a large bowl, mix together the tofu, cornstarch, salt, and pepper until well coated.
2. Preheat the air fryer to 400°F (200°C).
3. Place the tofu in a single layer in the air fryer basket. Cook for 10-15 minutes, flipping the tofu halfway through cooking, or until crispy and golden brown. Remove from the air fryer and set aside.
4. In a large wok or frying pan, heat the vegetable oil over high heat. Add the bell peppers, onion, garlic, and broccoli, and stir-fry for 2-3 minutes or until the vegetables are tender.
5. Add the crispy tofu to the pan, along with the soy sauce, hoisin sauce, and sesame oil. Stir-fry for an additional 2-3 minutes or until the sauce is well combined and the tofu is heated through.

Chapter 10: Sweet Treats and Desserts

Air-Fried Donut Holes

Serves: 4
Prep time: 15 minutes / Cook time: 8 minutes

Ingredients:
- 200g all-purpose flour
- 50g granulated sugar
- 2 tsp baking powder
- 1/4 tsp salt
- 120ml plant-based milk (such as almond or oat milk)
- 2 tbsp vegetable oil
- 1 tsp vanilla extract
- Oil spray
- Icing sugar, for dusting

Preparation instructions:
1. Preheat the Air Fryer to 180°C for 5 minutes.
2. In a bowl, whisk together flour, sugar, baking powder, and salt.
3. Add plant-based milk, vegetable oil, and vanilla extract to the dry Ingredients. Mix until just combined.
4. Lightly grease your hands with oil and shape the dough into small balls to form donut holes.
5. Place the donut holes in the air fryer basket, making sure they're not too crowded.
6. Air fry at 180°C for about 6-8 minutes, turning the donut holes halfway through, until they are golden and cooked through.
7. Remove from the air fryer and let them cool slightly.
8. Dust the donut holes with icing sugar before serving.

Cinnamon Sugar Apple Chips

Serves: 4
Prep time: 10 minutes / Cook time: 15 minutes

Ingredients:
- 2 apples, cored and thinly sliced
- 1 tbsp lemon juice
- 1 tsp ground cinnamon
- 2 tbsp granulated sugar

Preparation instructions:
1. Preheat the Air Fryer to 150°C for 5 minutes.
2. In a bowl, toss apple slices with lemon juice to prevent browning.
3. In a separate bowl, mix ground cinnamon and granulated sugar.
4. Dip each apple slice in the cinnamon-sugar mixture, coating both sides.
5. Place the coated apple slices in a single layer in the air fryer basket.
6. Air fry at 150°C for about 12-15 minutes, flipping the slices halfway through, until they are crispy.
7. Let the apple chips cool before enjoying.

Chocolate-Stuffed Crescent Rolls

Serves: 4
Prep time: 10 minutes / Cook time: 10 minutes

Ingredients:
- 1 tube of crescent roll dough (about 250g)
- 100g vegan chocolate chips

Preparation instructions:
1. Preheat the Air Fryer to 180°C for 5 minutes.
2. Unroll the crescent roll dough and separate into individual triangles.
3. Place a small handful of vegan chocolate chips at the wide end of each triangle.
4. Roll up the dough, enclosing the chocolate chips.
5. Place the stuffed crescent rolls in the air fryer basket.
6. Air fry at 180°C for about 8-10 minutes, until the rolls are golden and the chocolate is melted.
7. Allow the crescent rolls to cool slightly before serving.

Mixed Berry Hand Pies

Serves: 4
Prep time: 20 minutes / Cook time: 15 minutes

Ingredients:

- 200g mixed berries (such as strawberries, blueberries, and raspberries)
- 50g granulated sugar
- 1 tsp cornstarch
- 1 sheet of puff pastry, thawed
- 1 tbsp whole milk

Preparation instructions:

1. Preheat the Air Fryer to 180°C for 5 minutes.
2. In a bowl, mix mixed berries, granulated sugar, and cornstarch.
3. Roll out the puff pastry sheet and cut it into squares.
4. Place a spoonful of the berry mixture onto one half of each square.
5. Fold the other half of the square over the berries to create a triangle shape.
6. Press the edges to seal and crimp with a fork.
7. Brush the tops of the hand pies with milk. Place the hand pies in the air fryer basket.
8. Air fry at 180°C for about 12-15 minutes, until the pies are golden and flaky.
9. Allow the hand pies to cool slightly before enjoying.

Peach and Raspberry Crisp

Serves: 4
Prep time: 15 minutes / Cook time: 20 minutes

Ingredients:

- 300g sliced peaches (fresh or frozen)
- 150g raspberries (fresh or frozen)
- 50g granulated sugar
- 1 tsp lemon juice
- 60g rolled oats
- 40g all-purpose flour
- 40g brown sugar
- 1/2 tsp ground cinnamon
- 30g butter, melted

Preparation instructions:

1. Preheat the Air Fryer to 180°C for 5 minutes.
2. In a bowl, combine sliced peaches, raspberries, granulated sugar, and lemon juice.
3. In a separate bowl, mix rolled oats, all-purpose flour, brown sugar, ground cinnamon, and melted butter to make the crisp topping.
4. Divide the fruit mixture into individual ramekins.
5. Sprinkle the crisp topping over the fruit in each ramekin.
6. Place the ramekins in the air fryer basket.
7. Air fry at 180°C for about 15-18 minutes, until the topping is golden and the fruit is bubbling.
9. Allow the peach and raspberry crisps to cool slightly before serving.

Banana Nutella Spring Rolls

Serves: 4
Prep time: 15 minutes / Cook time: 8 minutes

Ingredients:

- 4 spring roll wrappers
- 2 bananas, sliced
- 4 tbsp Nutella or hazelnut spread
- Milk, for sealing

Preparation instructions:

1. Preheat the Air Fryer to 180°C for 5 minutes.
2. Lay out a spring roll wrapper with one corner pointing towards you.
3. Place banana slices in the centre of the wrapper.
4. Add a tablespoon of Nutella over the bananas.
5. Fold the sides of the wrapper towards the centre and roll tightly.
6. Use a bit of milk to seal the edge of the wrapper.
7. Repeat the process for the remaining wrappers. Place the spring rolls in the air fryer basket.
8. Air fry at 180°C for about 6-8 minutes, until the rolls are crispy and golden.
9. Let the banana Nutella spring rolls cool slightly before enjoying.

Mini Churros with Chocolate Sauce

Serves: 4
Prep time: 15 minutes / Cook time: 15 minutes

Ingredients:
* 200g all-purpose flour
* 2 tbsp granulated sugar
* 1/2 tsp salt
* 240 ml milk
* 60g butter
* 1 tsp vanilla extract
* Oil spray
* 100g chocolate chips
* 60ml cream

Preparation instructions:
1. Preheat the Air Fryer to 180°C for 5 minutes.
2. In a saucepan, combine milk, butter, granulated sugar, and salt. Heat over medium heat until the butter is melted.
3. Remove from heat and stir in all-purpose flour and vanilla extract until a smooth dough forms.
4. Transfer the dough to a piping bag fitted with a star tip.
5. Pipe strips of dough directly into the air fryer basket to form mini churros.
6. Air fry at 180°C for about 10-12 minutes, turning the churros halfway through, until they are golden and crispy.
7. In a separate bowl, melt chocolate chips and cream together to create the chocolate sauce.
8. Serve the mini churros with the chocolate sauce for dipping.

Coconut Macaroon Bites

Serves: 4
Prep time: 15 minutes / Cook time: 10 minutes

Ingredients:
* 200g shredded coconut
* 150ml condensed coconut milk
* 1 tsp vanilla extract
* 100g chocolate chips

Preparation instructions:
1. Preheat the Air Fryer to 160°C for 5 minutes.
2. In a bowl, combine shredded coconut, condensed coconut milk, and vanilla extract.
3. Form the mixture into small bite-sized balls.
4. Place the coconut macaroon bites in the air fryer basket.
5. Air fry at 160°C for about 8-10 minutes, until the macaroons are golden and toasted.
6. Allow the macaroon bites to cool slightly.
7. In a separate bowl, melt chocolate chips.
8. Dip the bottoms of the macaroon bites in the melted chocolate. Place the macaroon bites on parchment paper to let the chocolate set.
9. Enjoy the coconut macaroon bites as a delightful treat.

Nutty Chocolate-Stuffed Dates

Serves: 4
Prep time: 15 minutes / Cook time: 8 minutes

Ingredients:
* 16 large Medjool dates
* 60g dark chocolate, chopped
* 30g mixed nuts (such as almonds, walnuts, or hazelnuts), chopped

Preparation instructions:
1. Preheat the Air Fryer to 180°C for 5 minutes.
2. Carefully slit each date and remove the pit.
3. Stuff each date with a piece of chopped dark chocolate and a pinch of chopped mixed nuts.
4. Gently press the dates closed.
5. Place the stuffed dates in the air fryer basket.
6. Air fry at 180°C for about 6-8 minutes, until the chocolate is melted and the dates are slightly caramelised.
7. Let the nutty chocolate-stuffed dates cool slightly before enjoying.

Blueberry Lemon Pastry Bites

Serves: 4
Prep time: 15 minutes / Cook time: 12 minutes

Ingredients:

- 1 sheet of puff pastry, thawed
- 100g blueberries
- Zest of 1 lemon
- 2 tbsp granulated sugar
- 1 tbsp milk
- Icing sugar, for dusting

Preparation instructions:

1. Preheat the Air Fryer to 180°C for 5 minutes.
2. Roll out the puff pastry sheet and cut it into squares.
3. In a bowl, mix blueberries, lemon zest, and granulated sugar.
4. Place a spoonful of the blueberry mixture onto each puff pastry square.
5. Fold the pastry squares over the filling to create triangles.
6. Press the edges to seal and crimp with a fork.
7. Brush the tops of the pastry bites with milk. Place the pastry bites in the air fryer basket.
8. Air fry at 180°C for about 10-12 minutes, until the bites are golden and puffed.
9. Dust the blueberry lemon pastry bites with icing sugar before serving.

Strawberry Shortcake Biscuits

Serves: 4
Prep time: 15 minutes / Cook time: 12 minutes

Ingredients:

- 200g fresh strawberries, hulled and sliced
- 2 tbsp granulated sugar
- 1 sheet of puff pastry, thawed
- 1 tbsp milk
- Icing sugar, for dusting

Preparation instructions:

1. Preheat the Air Fryer to 180°C for 5 minutes.
2. In a bowl, mix sliced strawberries with granulated sugar. Let them macerate while you prepare the pastry.
3. Roll out the puff pastry sheet and cut it into squares.
4. Place a spoonful of the strawberry mixture onto the centre of each puff pastry square.
5. Fold the pastry squares over the strawberries to create turnovers.
6. Press the edges to seal and crimp with a fork.
7. Brush the tops of the turnovers with milk. Place the turnovers in the air fryer basket.
8. Air fry at 180°C for about 10-12 minutes, until the turnovers are golden and puffed.
9. Dust the strawberry shortcake turnovers with icing sugar before serving.

Mini S'mores Pies

Serves: 4
Prep time: 15 minutes / Cook time: 10 minutes

Ingredients:

- 1 sheet of puff pastry, thawed
- 16 mini marshmallows
- 30g chocolate, chopped
- 4 digestive biscuits, crushed into crumbs
- Icing sugar, for dusting

Preparation instructions:

1. Preheat the Air Fryer to 180°C for 5 minutes.
2. Roll out the puff pastry sheet and cut it into squares.
3. Place a small spoonful of crushed digestive biscuits in the centre of each pastry square.
4. Top with chopped chocolate and two mini marshmallows.
5. Fold the pastry squares over the filling to create mini pies.
6. Press the edges to seal and crimp with a fork.
7. Place the mini s'mores pies in the air fryer basket.
8. Air fry at 180°C for about 8-10 minutes, until

the pies are golden and the marshmallows are toasted.

9. Dust the mini s'mores pies with icing sugar before serving.

Caramelized Pineapple Rings

Serves: 4

Prep time: 10 minutes / Cook time: 8 minutes

Ingredients:

- 1 ripe pineapple, peeled and cored
- 50g brown sugar
- 1/2 tsp ground cinnamon

Preparation instructions:

1. Preheat the Air Fryer to 180°C for 5 minutes.
2. Slice the pineapple into rings, about 1 cm thick.
3. In a bowl, mix brown sugar and ground cinnamon.
4. Dip each pineapple ring into the sugar mixture, coating both sides.
5. Place the coated pineapple rings in the air fryer basket.
6. Air fry at 180°C for about 6-8 minutes, until the pineapple rings are caramelised and slightly golden.
7. Let the caramelised pineapple rings cool slightly before serving.

Raspberry Chocolate Turnovers

Serves: 4

Prep time: 15 minutes / Cook time: 12 minutes

Ingredients:

- 1 sheet of puff pastry, thawed
- 100g fresh raspberries
- 40g chocolate, chopped
- 2 tbsp granulated sugar
- 1 tbsp milk
- Icing sugar, for dusting

Preparation instructions:

1. Preheat the Air Fryer to 180°C for 5 minutes.
2. Roll out the puff pastry sheet and cut it into squares.
3. In a bowl, mix raspberries with granulated sugar.
4. Place a spoonful of the raspberry mixture onto each puff pastry square.
5. Sprinkle chopped chocolate over the raspberries.
6. Fold the pastry squares over the filling to create turnovers.
7. Press the edges to seal and crimp with a fork. Brush the tops of the turnovers with milk. Place the turnovers in the air fryer basket.
8. Air fry at 180°C for about 10-12 minutes, until the turnovers are golden and puffed.
9. Dust the raspberry chocolate turnovers with icing sugar before serving.

Maple Pecan Stuffed Apples

Serves: 4

Prep time: 15 minutes / Cook time: 12 minutes

Ingredients:

- 4 apples (such as Granny Smith), cored
- 40g pecans, chopped
- 2 tbsp maple syrup
- 1 tsp ground cinnamon

Preparation instructions:

1. Preheat the Air Fryer to 180°C for 5 minutes.
2. In a bowl, mix chopped pecans with maple syrup and ground cinnamon.
3. Stuff each cored apple with the pecan mixture.
4. Place the stuffed apples in the air fryer basket.
5. Air fry at 180°C for about 10-12 minutes, until the apples are tender and slightly caramelised.
6. Let the maple pecan stuffed apples cool slightly before serving.

Almond Joy-Stuffed Crepes

Serves: 4

Prep time: 15 minutes / Cook time: 12 minutes

Ingredients:

- 240g all-purpose flour
- 360 ml milk
- 2 tbsp granulated sugar

- 1 tsp vanilla extract
- 1/4 tsp salt
- 60g chocolate chips
- 50g shredded coconut
- 50g chopped almonds
- Oil spray
- Chocolate sauce, for drizzling

Preparation instructions:

1. Preheat the Air Fryer to 180°C for 5 minutes.
2. In a blender, combine all-purpose flour, milk, granulated sugar, vanilla extract, and salt. Blend until smooth.
3. Heat a non-stick skillet over medium heat and lightly grease with oil spray.
4. Pour a small amount of crepe batter into the skillet and swirl to coat the bottom evenly. Cook for about 1-2 minutes until the edges lift.
5. Flip the crepe and cook for an additional 1-2 minutes. Repeat with the remaining batter.
6. In a bowl, mix chocolate chips, shredded coconut, and chopped almonds.
7. Spoon the chocolate-coconut mixture onto half of each crepe and fold the other half over to create a half-moon shape. Place the stuffed crepes in the air fryer basket.
8. Air fry at 180°C for about 6-8 minutes, until the crepes are crispy and the chocolate is melted.
9. Drizzle the almond joy-stuffed crepes with plant-based chocolate sauce before serving.

Air Fryer Chocolate Chip Cookies

Serves: 6-8
Prep time: 10 mins / Cook time: 8-10 mins

Ingredients:

- 100g unsalted butter, softened
- 75g granulated sweetener
- 1 large egg
- 1 tsp vanilla extract
- 140g plain flour
- 1/2 tsp baking soda
- 1/4 tsp salt

- 80g Sugar-free chocolate chips

Preparation instructions:

1. Preheat the air fryer to 175°C.
2. In a mixing bowl, cream together the butter and sweetener until light and fluffy.
3. Beat in the egg and vanilla extract until well combined.
4. In another bowl, whisk together the flour, baking soda, and salt.
5. Gradually stir in the dry ingredients to the wet ingredients until a dough forms.
6. Fold in the chocolate chips.
7. Divide the dough into 6-8 equal-sized balls and place them in the air fryer basket.
8. Flatten each ball slightly with the palm of your hand.
9. Air fry for 8-10 minutes, or until golden brown and crispy on the outside.
10. Let the cookies cool on a wire rack before serving. Enjoy!

Apple and Mixed Berry Crumble (Diabetic-Friendly)

Serves: 4
Prep time: 15 mins Cook time: 15 - 20 mins

Ingredients:
Fruit Base
- 300 g apples
- 150 g mixed berries (frozen berries will work too)
- 50 g granulated sweetener
- 1 tsp cinnamon
- Crumble
- 200 g almond flour
- 100 g butter (soft)
- 50 g granulated sweetener
- 50 g oats

Served with Sugar-free whipped cream, low-Sugar ice cream or custard.

Preparation Instructions:

1. Peel apples and dice very finely.
2. Mix berries, apple slices, sweetener, and

cinnamon together.

3. Put the berry mix into your dish.
4. In a separate bowl, rub the almond flour and butter together until they have a crumbly texture.
5. Thoroughly mix the sweetener and oats into this mixture.
6. Spoon the crumble over the berry and apple.
7. Place the dish in the air fryer at 180°C for about 15 - 20 minutes. The crumble topping should have a golden glow to it.
8. Serve with a choice of Sugar-free whipped cream, low-Sugar ice cream or custard.

Lava cake with vanilla ice cream

Serves 3 cakes
Prep time: 10 minutes / Cook time: 3 minutes

Ingredients

- 75g milk chocolate chips
- 75g unsalted butter
- 1 egg
- A pinch of salt
- 40g plain flour
- Side
- Vanilla ice cream

Preparation instructions

1. Place a bowl with the chocolate and butter on top of the hot water bath.
2. Stir as the heat melts the mixture until smooth consistency.
3. Remove the bowl from the fire.
4. Beat the egg in a small bowl and add it to the chocolate mixture. Stir well.
5. Add in salt and flour and stir well till smooth.
6. Add a coat of butter to your air fryer containers to aid easy removal of your cakes later, and add the mixture to your containers.

7. Preheat the air fryer to 160C for 5 mins and cook for about 2 to 3 mins.
8. Remove it from the air fryer once you see that the top is cooked and looks solid.
9. Remove from the air fryer, flip it over, add the vanilla ice cream on the side or top and enjoy!

Brown Sugar Banana Bread

Serves 4
Prep time: 20 minutes / Cook time: 22-24 minutes

Ingredients

- 195 g packed light brown sugar
- 1 large egg, beaten
- 2 tablespoons unsalted butter, melted
- 120 ml milk, whole or semi-skimmed
- 250 g plain flour
- 1½ teaspoons baking powder
- 1 teaspoon ground cinnamon
- ½ teaspoon salt
- 1 banana, mashed
- 1 to 2 tablespoons coconut, or avocado oil oil
- 30 g icing sugar (optional)

Preparation instructions

1. In a large bowl, stir together the brown sugar, egg, melted butter, and milk.
2. In a medium bowl, whisk the flour, baking powder, cinnamon, and salt until blended. Add the flour mixture to the sugar mixture and stir just to blend.
3. Add the mashed banana and stir to combine.
4. Preheat the air fryer to 176°C. Spritz 2 mini loaf pans with oil.
5. Evenly divide the batter between the prepared pans and place them in the air fryer basket.
6. Cook for 22 to 24 minutes, or until a knife inserted into the middle of the loaves comes out clean.
7. Dust the warm loaves with icing sugar (if using).

Printed in Great Britain
by Amazon

30933976R00044